simply
ONE POT

Kate McMillan

Photography by Erin Kunkel

**FOG
CITY**

PRESS

FOG CITY PRESS

a division of Weldon Owen Inc.
1045 Sansome Street, Suite 100, San Francisco, CA 94111
www.weldonowen.com

SIMPLY ONE POT

Conceived and produced by Weldon Owen, Inc.
In collaboration with Williams-Sonoma, Inc.
3250 Van Ness Avenue, San Francisco, CA 94109

A WELDON OWEN PRODUCTION

Printed and bound in China by 1010 Printing, Ltd.

This book as been previously published as
Williams-Sonoma One Pot of the Day

This edition printed in 2014
10 9 8 7 6 5 4 3 2 1

Library of Congress Cataloging-in-Publication
data is available

ISBN 13: 978-1-61628-899-0
ISBN 10: 1-61628-899-X

weldonowen

President Roger Shaw
Senior VP, Sales and Marketing Amy Kaneko
Finance Director Philip Paulick

Associate Publisher Amy Marr
Associate Editor Emma Rudolph

Creative Director Kelly Booth
Designer Howie Severson
Senior Production Designer Rachel Lopez Metzger

Production Director Chris Hemesath
Associate Production Director Michelle Duggan

Photographer Erin Kunkel
Food Stylist Robyn Valarik
Prop Stylist Leigh Noe

Weldon Owen is a division of **BONNIER**

ACKNOWLEDGMENTS

Weldon Owen wishes to thank the following people for their generous support in producing
this book: David Bornfriend, Sarah Putman Clegg, Jane Tunks Demel, Judith Dunham, David Evans,
Lesli J. Neilson, Jennifer Newens, Elizabeth Parson, and Jason Wheeler

CONTENTS

A DISH FOR EVERY DAY

From gratins to casseroles, stir-fries to stews, tagines to curries—this collection of scrumptious recipes offers ease, comfort, and flavor for everyday cooking. Whether braised, baked, sautéed, or slow-cooked, you'll find inspired recipes that combine fresh ingredients into fantastic one-pot meals.

This colorful cookbook presents 70 main-course dishes organized by primary ingredient: vegetables, seafood, beef and veal, pork, lamb, and poultry. Each recipe is prepared or served in a pot, baking dish, or on a platter. Emphasizing versatility, this style of cooking allows you to make the most of your cooking time, mixing and matching ingredients and techniques to create delicious, interesting, and wholesome food that matches any occasion and season.

Flexible and adaptable, the one-pot approach saves time and makes for smart cooking. Drawing on favorite meats, seafood, and vegetables as a starting point, you'll learn how to craft an exceptional dish by simply adding potatoes, grains, fresh produce, and seasoning, varying the cooking technique and flavor profile. Recipes like Arroz Con Pollo, Vietnamese Clay Pot Fish, and Summer Coq Au Vin draw on international cuisines and are satisfying enough to make a full meal; other dishes, such as smoked salmon frittata, beef and basil stir-fry, and pork medallions with roasted nectarines may need only a green salad, a pot of steamed rice, or a loaf of crusty bread to feed and nourish the whole family.

In these pages, you'll find comforting classics like beef bourguignon and macaroni and cheese as well as contemporary fare—rigatoni baked with fennel, sausage, and pepperonata; calamari stir-fried with pea shoots; pork chops braised with cherries; and pan-fried steak piperade. There are also numerous meatless offerings, from light and elegant to hearty and filling, that feature easy-to-prepare grains or proteins paired with garden-based ingredients and enticing flavors: vegetarian enchiladas; spinach-feta quiche; baked pasta primavera; and cheesey polenta with roasted vegetables.

With this vast collection of recipes as your guide, and gorgeous color photographs to illustrate the way, you're sure to find the perfect one-pot dish to make any night of the week.

VEGETABLES

BAKED PASTA PRIMAVERA

Colorful zucchini, yellow squash, and cherry tomatoes nestle in this creamy pasta. Lemon zest brightens the dish, and fresh bread crumbs on top add a delightful crunch. Cut all the vegetables to about the same size to ensure that they cook evenly. Substitute other seasonal vegetables to make this recipe year-round.

serves 6

2 Tbsp olive oil, plus more for greasing

½ yellow onion, chopped

3 cloves garlic, minced

2 small yellow summer squash, cut into ¾-inch (2-cm) pieces

2 small zucchini, cut into ¾-inch (2-cm) pieces

1 large carrot, cut into ¾-inch (2-cm) matchsticks

Salt and freshly ground pepper

1 cup (6 oz/185 g) small cherry tomatoes

¾ lb (375 g) gemelli pasta, cooked according to the package directions

1 Tbsp unsalted butter

1 tsp grated lemon zest

1 Tbsp all-purpose flour

1 cup (8 fl oz/250 ml) milk

1 cup (4 oz/125 g) grated Parmesan cheese

2 Tbsp cream cheese

1 cup (4 oz/125 g) shredded mozzarella cheese

1 cup (2 oz/60 g) fresh bread crumbs

Preheat the oven to 400°F (200°C). Oil a 9-by-13-inch (23-by-33-cm) baking dish.

In a large frying pan, heat the 2 Tbsp oil over medium-high heat. Add the onion and two-thirds of the garlic and sauté until translucent, about 4 minutes. Add the squash, zucchini, and carrot, and season with salt and pepper. Sauté until the vegetables are very soft and just beginning to brown, about 5 minutes. Add the tomatoes and cook just until they start to soften but still hold their shape, about 3 minutes. Transfer to a bowl and add the cooked pasta.

In a small saucepan, melt the butter over medium heat. Add the remaining garlic and the lemon zest and sauté just until the garlic softens, about 2 minutes, being careful not to burn the garlic. Add the flour and cook, stirring constantly, for 1 minute. Slowly add the milk and bring to a simmer. Reduce the heat to low and cook, stirring frequently, until thickened, 4–5 minutes. Add ¾ cup (3 oz/90 g) of the Parmesan and the cream cheese and whisk until the cheeses melt. Season with salt and pepper.

Pour the cream sauce into the bowl with the pasta and the vegetables and toss to combine. Transfer to the prepared dish. Sprinkle with the mozzarella, the remaining Parmesan, and the bread crumbs.

Bake until the pasta is warmed through and the bread crumbs are golden brown, about 15 minutes. Spoon onto plates and serve.

Quiche was traditionally offered as a first course, but now it is more commonly served as a main course at brunch or lunchtime. Take it into dinner with healthy greens and tangy feta cheese. Spinach particularly complements the rich egg custard and flaky pastry crust.

SPINACH-FETA QUICHE

serves 8

FOR THE TART DOUGH

1⅓ cups (7 oz/220 g) all-purpose flour

1 Tbsp sugar

Salt

½ cup (4 oz/125 g) cold unsalted butter, cut into small pieces

4 Tbsp (2 fl oz/60 ml) ice water, or more as needed

1 cup (1 oz/30 g) steamed fresh spinach or thawed frozen spinach, drained and squeezed completely dry

3 eggs

Salt and freshly ground pepper

Pinch of grated nutmeg

¾ cup (6 fl oz/180 ml) heavy cream

¾ cup (6 fl oz/180 ml) milk

1 cup (5 oz/155 g) crumbled feta cheese

1 Tbsp unsalted butter, cut into ¼-inch (6-mm) pieces

To make the tart dough, in a food processor, combine the flour, sugar, and ¼ tsp salt. Pulse to mix. Add the butter and pulse 8 times. Add the 4 Tbsp ice water and pulse about 10 times. If the dough crumbles, add more ice water, a Tbsp at a time, and pulse just until the dough holds together. Transfer the dough to a floured work surface, shape into a 6-inch (15-cm) disk, wrap in plastic wrap, and refrigerate for at least 1 hour or up to overnight.

Preheat the oven to 400°F (200°C). On a floured work surface, roll out the dough into a round about 10½ inches (26.5 cm) in diameter and ¼ inch (6 mm) thick. Carefully transfer it to a 9-inch (23-cm) quiche pan or other straight-sided pan with 1-inch (2.5-cm) sides. Press the dough into the bottom and sides of the pan. Pinch the dough around the rim to form a fluted edge.

Line the dough with foil and fill with pie weights or dried beans. Bake until the crust is dry, about 15 minutes. Remove from the oven and lift out the weights and foil. Transfer to a wire rack. Reduce the oven temperature to 350°F (180°C) and set a rack in the bottom third of the oven.

Arrange the spinach evenly in the prebaked crust. In a large bowl, whisk together the eggs, ½ tsp salt, ⅛ tsp pepper, and the nutmeg. Add the cream and milk and whisk until well blended. Slowly pour the egg mixture over the spinach in the crust. Dot the top with the cheese and the butter.

Bake on the bottom oven rack until the top is lightly browned and the filling is just barely set, 40–45 minutes. Transfer to the wire rack and let stand for 5 minutes. Cut into wedges and serve.

*Spanakopita
is a marvelous
picnic or potluck
contender. Layers
of flaky filo (found
in the freezer
aisle) enclose the
familiar spinach
and feta filling.
The whole pan is
easy to transport
and cut into neat
little squares,
which will be tasty
either warm or at
room temperature.*

SPANAKOPITA

serves 6

2 lb (1 kg) spinach, tough stems removed

5 Tbsp (3 fl oz/80 ml) olive oil

**½ cup (1½ oz/45 g) chopped green onions,
white and tender green tops**

⅓ cup (2½ oz/75 g) small-curd cottage cheese

½ cup (2 oz/60 g) crumbled feta cheese

¼ cup (⅓ oz/10 g) chopped fresh dill

¼ cup (⅓ oz/10 g) chopped fresh flat-leaf parsley

1 egg, beaten

⅛ tsp grated nutmeg

Salt and freshly ground pepper

16 sheets frozen filo dough, thawed

Preheat the oven to 350°F (180°C). Have ready an 8-inch (20-cm) square baking dish.

Put the spinach in a large sauté pan, cover, and cook over medium heat, stirring several times, until just tender, about 3 minutes. Drain, spread the spinach on a plate to cool, and then squeeze to remove the excess liquid. Finely chop the spinach, put it in a large bowl, and set aside. Wipe out the pan.

Return the pan to medium-high heat, and warm 1 Tbsp of the oil. Add the green onions and sauté until softened, about 3 minutes. Add to the spinach. Add the cottage cheese, feta, dill, parsley, egg, and nutmeg to the bowl. Using a fork, toss to combine well. Season with salt and pepper.

Lay the filo on a dry kitchen towel. Cover with a sheet of plastic wrap, then with a dampened kitchen towel. Place 1 filo sheet on a work surface. Brush lightly with some of the remaining 4 Tbsp (2 fl oz/60 ml) oil, working from the edges to the center. Layer 7 more sheets over the first, lightly oiling each one. Using a sharp knife, trim the stacked sheets into an 8½-inch (21.5-cm) square. Fit the dough stack into the bottom and slightly up the sides of the baking dish.

Spoon the filling into the pan to cover the filo. Using the remaining filo, make another stack of 8 sheets in the same way and trim into an 8-inch (20-cm) square. Place the second stack to cover the spinach filling. Using the knife, cut through the pie, dividing it in half. Turn the pan 90 degrees and cut the pie into thirds to make 6 pieces.

Bake until the filo is crisp and golden, about 45 minutes. Transfer to a wire rack and let cool for about 20 minutes before serving.

RISOTTO WITH TALEGGIO, RADICCHIO & RED WINE

In this refined and beautifully colored risotto, pleasantly bitter radicchio is balanced by creamy Taleggio cheese, which melts readily, making it a good option to stir into risotto or polenta. Gently swirl in the cheese just before serving.

serves 6

2 cups (16 fl oz/500 ml) *each* chicken broth and beef broth
or 4 cups (32 fl oz/1 l) vegetable broth

1 Tbsp olive oil

2 cups (6 oz/185 g) shredded radicchio (about 1 small head)

2 Tbsp unsalted butter

½ yellow onion, finely chopped

2 cups (14 oz/440 g) Arborio or Carnaroli rice

2 cups (16 fl oz/500 ml) dry red wine

6 oz (185 g) Taleggio cheese, rind removed, cut into small pieces

Salt and freshly ground pepper

⅓ cup (1½ oz/45 g) walnuts, toasted and chopped (optional)

Chopped fresh flat-leaf parsley for garnish (optional)

In a saucepan, bring the chicken and beef broths to a gentle simmer over medium heat. Reduce the heat to low and maintain a simmer.

In a large, heavy saucepan, warm the olive oil over medium-high heat. Add the radicchio and sauté until the edges are golden, about 4 minutes. Drain on paper towels.

In the large saucepan, melt 1 Tbsp of the butter over medium-high heat. Add the onion and sauté until translucent, about 5 minutes. Add the rice and stir until well coated with butter and translucent, about 2 minutes. Add the wine, a little at a time, and cook, stirring constantly, until nearly absorbed, 5–6 minutes.

Reduce the heat to medium and start adding the simmering broth to the rice a ladleful at a time, stirring frequently after each addition. Wait until the broth is almost completely absorbed (but the rice is never dry on top) before adding the next ladleful. After about 20 minutes, the rice will be tender to the bite and creamy.

Stir in the sautéed radicchio, the remaining 1 Tbsp butter, and the cheese. Season with salt and pepper. Spoon into bowls, top with the walnuts and parsley, if using, and serve.

RISOTTO WITH FRESH CORN & BASIL OIL

Corn lovers eagerly anticipate its arrival at markets during the summer. Purists insist on cooking corn on the cob only until warmed through, either boiled or steamed, to preserve its sweetness and crunch. Cut from the cob, the fresh kernels are added raw to this creamy risotto, and cook in the gentle heat. A drizzle of basil oil provides a distinctive finish.

serves 4

¼ cup (⅓ oz/10 g) fresh basil, chopped

¼ cup (2 fl oz/60 ml) extra-virgin olive oil

5 cups (40 fl oz/1.25 l) chicken broth

2 Tbsp unsalted butter

1 cup (3 oz/90 g) thinly sliced leeks, white and pale green parts

1½ cups (10 oz/315 g) Arborio or Carnaroli rice

Kernels from 2 or 3 ears of corn

Salt and freshly ground pepper

2 Tbsp minced fresh chives

In a blender, combine the basil and olive oil and process until combined. Set aside.

In a saucepan, bring the broth to a gentle simmer over medium heat. Reduce the heat to low and maintain a simmer.

In a large, heavy saucepan, melt the butter over medium heat. Add the leeks, stir to coat, cover, reduce the heat to medium-low, and cook until translucent, about 5 minutes. Raise the heat to medium, add the rice, and stir until translucent, about 3 minutes. Add the simmering broth a ladleful at a time, stirring frequently after each addition. Wait until the broth is almost completely absorbed (but the rice is never dry on top) before adding the next ladleful. After 10 minutes, stir in the corn. After about 20 minutes, the rice should be tender to the bite and creamy. If you need more liquid, use heated water. Season with salt and pepper.

Remove from the heat and stir in the chives and 2 Tbsp of the basil oil. Divide among bowls, drizzle with more basil oil, and serve.

GOLDEN BEET & BLUE CHEESE RISOTTO

serves 4

¾ lb (375 g) golden or pink beets

Salt and freshly ground pepper

5 cups (40 fl oz/1.25 l) chicken or vegetable broth

3 Tbsp unsalted butter

1 small yellow onion, finely chopped

1½ cups (10½ oz/330 g) Arborio or Carnaroli rice

½ cup (4 fl oz/125 ml) dry white wine

⅓ cup (1 oz/30 g) grated Parmesan cheese

¼ cup (1½ oz/45 g) crumbled blue cheese

When root vegetables start to pile high at the farmers' market, seek out golden beets. Exceptionally sweet, they won't stain as much as their dark garnet cousins, which helps to preserve the pretty color of this risotto. Blue cheese complements the earthiness of this dish.

Preheat the oven to 400°F (200°C). Put the beets in a baking dish with water to cover the bottom of the dish. Cover tightly with foil and bake until the beets are tender when pierced with a fork, 40–60 minutes. Uncover and let cool. Cut off the beet tops and root ends. Peel the beets and cut into bite-sized pieces. Season with salt.

In a saucepan, bring the broth to a gentle simmer over medium heat and maintain over low heat.

In a large, heavy pot, melt 2 Tbsp of the butter over medium heat. Add the onion and a pinch of salt and sauté until the onion is soft, about 8 minutes. Add the rice and stir until translucent and coated with butter, about 3 minutes. Add the wine and stir until completely absorbed. Add a ladleful of the broth and simmer vigorously, stirring often, until the liquid is almost absorbed. Add another ladleful of broth. Continue simmering, stirring, and adding more broth until the rice is tender, about 25 minutes.

Stir in the beets and heat through, about 1 minute. Stir in the remaining 1 Tbsp butter and the cheeses. Let stand for 2 minutes. Season with salt and pepper and serve.

ROASTED PUMPKIN WITH GARLIC, SWEET POTATOES & CHERRY TOMATOES

serves 4

1 small sugar pumpkin or other winter squash

2 sweet potatoes

2 red onions

⅔ cup (5 fl oz/16 ml) olive oil

5 sprigs fresh thyme

1 head garlic, halved crosswise

2 Tbsp fresh lemon juice

2 tsp maple syrup

Salt and freshly ground pepper

1 pint grape or cherry tomatoes

Preheat the oven to 400°F (200°C). Cut the pumpkin into quarters and remove and discard the pulp and seeds (alternately, rinse and roast the seeds separately and use to garnish the dish later). Cut each pumpkin quarter into 3 wedges. Quarter the sweet potatoes lengthwise. Peel the onions and cut into wedges.

Place the pumpkin, sweet potatoes, and onions in a large mixing bowl. Add the oil, thyme, garlic, lemon juice, maple syrup, 1 tsp salt, and ½ tsp pepper. Toss to mix well and then spread out in a large roasting pan or on a baking sheet lined with parchment paper. Roast for 40–45 minutes, until all the vegetables are cooked through and golden brown, about 45 minutes.

Add the cherry tomatoes to the roasting pan, toss to coat with olive oil, and return the roasting pan to the oven for about 15 minutes more or until the tomatoes just begin to soften and release their juices. Sprinkle with salt and serve directly from the pan.

This fragrant
Moroccan stew,
or tagine,
combines winter
squash, sweet
potato, onion,
and carrot with
an aromatic blend
of spices and
the sweetness of
dried currants
and honey.
It is traditionally
cooked in
a shallow
earthenware pot
with a conical top,
but a Dutch oven
or other heavy pot
can be substituted.
Butternut squash
is the ideal winter
squash for this
dish, as it contains
less water than
many other types.

SPICED SQUASH TAGINE

serves 6

6–8 saffron threads

2 Tbsp olive oil

1 large yellow onion, finely chopped

1 tsp ground ginger

½ tsp ground cinnamon

½ tsp ground turmeric

1 butternut squash, about 1¼ lb (625 g), peeled, seeded, and cut into 1-inch (2.5-cm) cubes

1 large carrot, cut into slices ½ inch (12 mm) thick

1 large tomato, halved, seeded, and chopped

3 Tbsp dried currants

1 Tbsp honey

Salt and freshly ground pepper

1 large sweet potato, about ½ lb (250 g)

In a small bowl, combine the saffron with 1 Tbsp warm water and let soak for about 10 minutes.

In a large, heavy pot, heat the oil over medium-high heat. Add the onion and cook, stirring often, until softened, about 5 minutes. Stir in the ginger, cinnamon, and turmeric and cook, stirring often, until the spices are fragrant, about 30 seconds. Add the squash, carrot, tomato, currants, honey, and saffron with its soaking liquid. Pour in ¾ cup (6 fl oz/180 ml) water. Season with salt and pepper. Bring to a boil, reduce the heat to medium, cover, and simmer for about 10 minutes.

Peel the sweet potato, halve lengthwise, and then cut each half crosswise into slices ¾ inch (2 cm) thick. Add to the pot and cook, covered, until the vegetables are tender but still hold their shape, about 25 minutes. Serve directly from the pot.

TRUFFLED MAC & CHEESE

serves 6

Salt and freshly ground pepper

1 lb (500 g) elbow macaroni

2 tsp truffle oil

4 Tbsp (2 oz/60 g) butter, plus more for greasing

¼ cup (1½ oz/45 g) all-purpose flour

½ tsp sweet paprika

½ tsp Dijon mustard

2 cups (16 fl oz/500 ml) milk

1 cup (8 fl oz/250 ml) half-and-half

1½ cups (6 oz/185 g) shredded Gruyère cheese

1½ cups (6 oz/185 g) shredded white Cheddar cheese

2 Tbsp minced chives

Preheat the oven to 375°F (190°C). Butter a 9-by-13-inch (23-by-33-cm) baking dish.

Bring a large saucepan of salted water to a boil. Add the macaroni and cook, stirring occasionally, until not quite al dente, about 2 minutes less than the package directions. Drain and transfer to a large bowl. While the pasta is still warm, drizzle with the truffle oil and stir well.

Add the butter to the saucepan and melt it over medium-high heat. Add the flour, paprika, and mustard and cook, stirring well, until no visible flour remains, 1–3 minutes. Whisk in the milk, half-and-half, and a generous pinch of salt and bring to a boil. Simmer, whisking frequently to smooth out any lumps, for 4–5 minutes. Remove from the heat. Add a pinch of pepper and 1 cup (4 oz/125 g) each of the Gruyère and Cheddar. Stir until smooth.

Pour the cheese sauce onto the macaroni, add the chives, and mix well. Transfer to the prepared dish and top with the remaining cheeses. Bake until the top is lightly browned and the sauce is bubbly, 25–30 minutes. Let stand for 5 minutes before serving.

SPICY SIMMERED EGGS WITH KALE

serves 4

2 Tbsp unsalted butter

4 green onions, white and light green parts only, chopped

2 cloves garlic, minced

2 bunches kale, tough stems removed, roughly chopped

1 cup chicken or vegetable broth

Salt and freshly ground pepper

Zest and juice of 1 lemon

4 eggs

Red pepper flakes

In a large skillet over medium-high heat, melt the butter. Add the green onions and garlic and cook, stirring, until fragrant, about 1 minute. Add half of the kale and sauté, stirring frequently until it begins to wilt, about 2 minutes. Stir in the remaining kale and repeat. Add the chicken broth, ½ tsp salt, and ¼ tsp pepper. Stir in the lemon zest and juice. Let simmer, stirring occasionally, until the kale softens, about 6 minutes.

Using the back of a spoon, create a pocket for each egg in the kale. Crack one egg into each pocket. Reduce the heat to medium-low, and sprinkle the eggs with salt and pepper. Cover the pan and let the eggs cook until almost opaque, 4–5 minutes. Turn off the heat and let the eggs rest, covered, until done to taste. Sprinkle with red pepper flakes and serve.

BAKED EGGPLANT PARMESAN

serves 4

Replace chicken or veal with fleshy eggplant for a satisfying meatless meal. Dredging and panfrying the eggplant slices adds crunch and flavor, before smothering them in the pan with spicy marinara sauce. Serve with a big green salad.

FOR THE SPICY TOMATO SAUCE

2 Tbsp olive oil

4 large cloves garlic, chopped

4 cans (28 oz/875 g each) diced tomatoes, drained

1 tsp red pepper flakes

Salt and freshly ground pepper

2 Tbsp olive oil, plus more for dish

1 egg, beaten with 1 Tbsp water

½ cup (2 oz/60 g) dried bread crumbs

½ tsp dried oregano

2 Tbsp grated Parmesan cheese

Salt and freshly ground pepper

2 small eggplants, about 1½ lb (750 g) total, each cut crosswise into 8 slices

1 cup (4 oz/125 g) shredded mozzarella cheese

To make the spicy tomato sauce, in a large saucepan, heat the oil over medium heat. Add the garlic and sauté for 1 minute. Add the tomatoes and red pepper flakes, raise the heat to high, and bring to a boil. Reduce the heat to medium-low and simmer, uncovered, until the sauce is thick, about 40 minutes. Season with salt and pepper. Let cool slightly. Measure out 2 cups (16 fl oz/500 ml) of the sauce and set aside. Save the remaining sauce for another use.

Preheat the oven to 400°F (200°C). Lightly oil a 9-by-13-inch (23-by-33-cm) baking dish.

Put the egg mixture in a wide, shallow dish. Put the bread crumbs in another dish and stir in the oregano, Parmesan, ½ tsp salt, and ⅛ tsp pepper.

In a large frying pan, warm 1 Tbsp of the oil over medium-high heat. Working with 4 eggplant slices at a time, dip each slice in the egg mixture, letting the excess drip back into the bowl. Coat both sides with the bread crumbs and cook, turning once, until browned, about 6 minutes. Repeat with the remaining 1 Tbsp oil and remaining eggplant. Transfer to a plate.

Spoon one-third of the reserved sauce over the bottom of the prepared dish. Arrange half of the eggplant slices in a single layer on the sauce. Spoon one-third of the sauce onto the slices and sprinkle with half of the mozzarella. Top with the remaining eggplant slices and cover with the remaining sauce and mozzarella.

Bake until the eggplant is tender and the cheese is lightly browned and melted, about 15 minutes. Divide among plates and serve.

POLENTA WITH FONTINA & ROASTED VEGETABLES

serves 6

Bake a pan of polenta until it gets crispy at the edges, and then top it with anything your heart desires. Here, roasted summer vegetables pair with fontina, a mild melting cheese. But this is a fantastic recipe all year long: try it in the fall or winter with butternut squash, mushrooms, and Gorgonzola. Serve this dish with a salad of baby greens.

3 Tbsp olive oil, plus more for pans

1 small eggplant, cut into ¾-inch (2-cm) pieces

2 small zucchini, cut into ¾-inch (2-cm) pieces

2 small yellow summer squash, cut into ¾-inch (2-cm) pieces

½ red onion, cut into ¾-inch (2-cm) pieces

1 orange bell pepper, seeded and cut into ¾-inch (2-cm) pieces

Salt and freshly ground pepper

1 cup (7 oz/220 g) stone-ground polenta

2 Tbsp unsalted butter

1 cup (4 oz/125 g) grated Parmesan cheese

2 cups (8 oz/250 g) shredded fontina cheese

Preheat the oven to 450°F (230°C). Oil a rimmed baking sheet and an 8-inch (20-cm) baking dish.

In a large bowl, combine the eggplant, zucchini, summer squash, red onion, and bell pepper. Drizzle with the 3 Tbsp oil, season with salt and pepper, and toss to combine. Arrange in a single layer on the prepared baking sheet. Roast, tossing once, until the vegetables are caramelized, 20–25 minutes. Set aside. Reduce the oven temperature to 350°F (180°C).

Meanwhile, in a heavy saucepan, bring 4 cups (32 fl oz/1 l) salted water to a boil over medium heat. Stirring constantly, very slowly add the polenta. Cook, stirring constantly, until the polenta begins to thicken, about 5 minutes. Reduce the heat to low and continue to cook the polenta, stirring frequently, until the polenta is soft, about 25 minutes. Add the butter, Parmesan, and fontina and stir until the cheeses melt. Pour the polenta into the prepared baking dish and smooth the top.

Bake just until the polenta begins to set, about 15 minutes. Remove from the oven and top evenly with the roasted vegetables. Continue to bake until the vegetables are heated through, about 15 minutes. Serve the polenta directly from the dish.

This is a virtuous vegetarian supper, with nutrients from the cabbage and spinach, and protein from the tofu. The steaming technique is quick and lean, limiting the fat content to the healthy fats from coconut milk and peanut butter in the rich sauce.

STEAMED TOFU WITH GREENS & PEANUT SAUCE

serves 4

½ cup (5 oz/155 g) creamy peanut butter

½ cup (4 fl oz/125 ml) light coconut milk

3 Tbsp lime juice

2 Tbsp firmly packed golden brown sugar

1½ Tbsp soy sauce

1½–2 tsp Asian red chile paste

¾ lb (375 g) chopped green or savoy cabbage

6 oz (185 g) baby spinach

1 lb (500 g) firm tofu, cut into slices ½ inch (12 mm) thick

In a blender, combine the peanut butter, coconut milk, lime juice, brown sugar, soy sauce, and chile paste and process until smooth. Transfer the peanut sauce to a bowl.

Set a steamer rack inside a large pot filled with about 2 inches (5 cm) of water. Arrange the cabbage on the steamer and bring the water to a boil. Cover the pot and steam until the cabbage is wilted, about 7 minutes. Place the spinach leaves and tofu on top of the cabbage. Cover and steam until the spinach is wilted and the tofu is heated through, about 5 minutes longer.

Mound the cabbage, spinach, and tofu on a platter, drizzle with the peanut sauce, and serve.

BAKED ZUCCHINI & TOMATO TIAN

serves 4–6

2 Tbsp olive oil, plus more for dish

1 red onion, sliced

Salt and freshly ground pepper

¾ lb (375 g) plum tomatoes, sliced

2 small zucchini, about ¾ lb (375 g), sliced

1 Tbsp minced fresh basil

1 Tbsp minced fresh marjoram

¼ cup (2 fl oz/60 ml) chicken broth or water

Preheat the oven to 350°F (180°C). Oil a shallow 2-qt (2-l) baking dish.

In a frying pan, heat the 2 Tbsp oil over medium heat. Add the onion and sauté until soft, about 10 minutes. Transfer the onion to the prepared dish and spread evenly over the bottom. Season with salt and pepper.

Arrange the tomato and zucchini slices over the onion in alternate rows. Sprinkle with the basil and marjoram and season with salt and pepper. Pour the broth evenly over the top.

Cover with foil and bake until the vegetables are bubbling and tender, about 40 minutes. Remove from the oven and serve.

VEGETABLE ENCHILADAS

serves 4–6

12 corn tortillas, each 8 inches (20 cm) in diameter

2 Tbsp canola oil

Salt

1 cup (4 oz/125 g) shredded Monterey jack cheese

1 cup (4 oz/125 g) shredded white Cheddar cheese

2 cups (12 oz/375 g) fresh or thawed frozen corn kernels

2 zucchini, halved lengthwise and thinly sliced

1 large yellow onion, halved and thinly sliced

2 jars (12½ oz/390 g each) tomatillo salsa

¼ cup (2 oz/60 g) Mexican crema or sour cream

Preheat the oven to 300°F (150°C). Brush the tortillas with the oil, sprinkle with salt, and arrange on a baking sheet. Bake until warm and softened, about 1 minute. Remove from the oven and increase the oven temperature to 375°F (190°C).

In a small bowl, stir together half of the Monterey jack cheese, half of the Cheddar cheese, the corn, zucchini, and onion. Cover the bottom of a 9-by-13-inch (23-by-33-cm) baking dish with 1 jar of the salsa.

To assemble the enchiladas, place a tortilla on a work surface, add a few tablespoons of the vegetable filling down the center, and roll up the tortilla. Place it, seam side down, in the baking dish. Repeat with the remaining tortillas and filling. Spread the remaining jar of salsa over the top and sprinkle with the remaining cheese.

Cover the dish with foil and bake until the vegetables are tender and the cheese has melted, about 20 minutes. Uncover and continue to bake until the cheese is golden, 10–15 minutes. Let stand briefly before serving. Pass the crema at the table.

WINTER VEGETABLE COCONUT CURRY

serves 4

Coconut milk lends richness and exotic flavor to these creamy braised vegetables. It echoes the sweetness of both the root vegetables and squash, while taming the spicy red curry paste, pungent Asian fish sauce, and bright lime and cilantro that season the broth. Serve over cooked brown rice.

2 tsp canola oil

1 clove garlic, minced

¼-inch (6-mm) slice peeled fresh ginger, grated

2 tsp Thai red curry paste

1 tsp Asian fish sauce

1 sweet potato, about ½ lb (250 g), peeled and cut into ½-inch (12-mm) chunks

1 celery root, about ½ lb (250 g), peeled and cut into ½-inch (12-mm) chunks

3 cups (24 fl oz/750 ml) unsweetened coconut milk

1 delicata squash, about ½ lb (250 g), peeled and cut into ½-inch (12-mm) chunks

2 limes

2 Tbsp finely chopped fresh cilantro for garnish

In a saucepan, heat the oil over medium heat. Add the garlic and ginger and sauté until fragrant but not browned, about 1 minute. Add the curry paste and cook, stirring, for 1 minute. Add the fish sauce, sweet potato, and celery root and stir to combine. Reduce the heat to medium-low, pour in the coconut milk, and cook, stirring occasionally, for 10 minutes. Add the squash and cook until the vegetables are just tender but not falling apart, 12–15 minutes.

Meanwhile, finely grate the zest from the lime, then cut each lime into wedges. Stir the lime zest into the vegetables.

Serve, sprinkled with cilantro and topped with lime wedges.

SEAFOOD

Here, elegantly
ridged morels
partner with
smoky bacon and
caramelized leeks,
for a sophisticated
baked fish dish.
Just a touch
of champagne
vinegar adds
punch, and a few
snips of fresh
chives add color.

BAKED COD WITH LEEKS, MORELS & BACON

serves 4

¾ oz (20 g) dried morel mushrooms

½ cup (4 fl oz/125 ml) boiling water

3 Tbsp unsalted butter

4 slices bacon

2 cups (6 oz/185 g) thinly sliced leeks,
white and pale green parts

Salt and freshly ground pepper

1 tsp champagne vinegar

4 cod fillets, about 6 oz (185 g) each

1 Tbsp minced fresh chives

Preheat the oven to 375°F (190°C).

In a small heatproof bowl, soak the mushrooms in the boiling water for 20 minutes. Squeeze dry and roughly chop the larger mushrooms into bite-sized pieces. Set aside.

Melt 2 Tbsp of the butter in a large ovenproof frying pan over medium-high heat. Add the bacon and fry until crispy, about 5 minutes. Drain on paper towels. Pour off all but 3 Tbsp fat from the pan. Add the leeks and ¼ tsp salt, stir until evenly coated with the fat, and cook, stirring often, until tender and beginning to brown, about 10 minutes. Crumble the bacon and add half to the leeks along with the reserved morels and the vinegar. Toss to combine well and spread the leek mixture over the bottom of the pan.

Season the cod fillets with salt and pepper and lay them on top of the leeks. Dot with the remaining 1 Tbsp butter. Bake until the fish flakes with a fork, about 12 minutes. Garnish with the remaining bacon and the chives, and serve.

COD, LEEK & POTATO GRATIN

serves 4

Potatoes doused in creamy sauce are always comforting, but the addition of firm white fish and sweet, oniony leeks make this a dish fit for company. Toss together a big salad, open a bottle of dry white wine, and dinner is served.

Butter for dish

1½ lb (750 g) white potatoes, peeled

2 leeks, white and pale green parts, halved

1 lb (500 g) cod or haddock fillets, thickly sliced on the diagonal

Salt and ground pepper

1 cup (8 fl oz/250 ml) heavy cream

Preheat the oven to 375°F (190°C). Butter a 13-inch (33-cm) oval gratin pan or 4 deep, individual-sized baking dishes. Cut the potatoes crosswise into thin, uniform slices. Cut the leeks crosswise into slices about twice as thick as the potatoes. Season the fish lightly with salt and pepper.

Arrange half of the potato slices in the prepared dish, overlapping them to cover the bottom. Season lightly with salt and pepper. Scatter half of the leeks over the potatoes, then arrange the fish slices over the leeks in a single layer, overlapping the slices as necessary. Top with the remaining leeks, then with the remaining potatoes. Season with salt and pepper. Pour the cream evenly over the layers. Bake for 40 minutes.

Remove from the oven and spoon some of the cooking liquid over the top of the gratin to moisten the potatoes and help them brown. Continue to bake until the top layer of potatoes is tender when pierced with a sharp knife, about 20 minutes. Let stand for 10–15 minutes and serve.

ROCKFISH BRAISED WITH FENNEL & ONIONS

Roasting a whole fish creates an impressive one-pot meal. A scattering of thinly slivered vegetables cook quickly in the same pan. To prepare fennel for cooking, first trim the bulb of any browned bits. Cut off the long stalks and use only the bulb, trimming away the base of the core if it is thick and tough. Halve the bulb crosswise then cut into thin lengthwise slices.

serves 4

3 Tbsp olive oil

1 yellow onion, sliced

3 ribs celery, sliced

2 carrots, peeled, halved lengthwise, and sliced

1 small fennel bulb, trimmed and thinly sliced *(left)*

2 cloves garlic, minced

2 Tbsp chopped fresh dill, plus sprigs for garnish

Salt and freshly ground pepper

1 rockfish, about 2 lb (1 kg), cleaned

1 cup (8 fl oz/250 ml) dry white wine

Preheat the oven to 400°F (200°C).

In a large frying pan, warm the oil over medium-high heat. Add the onion, celery, carrot, fennel, and garlic and sauté until soft, about 5 minutes. Stir in the chopped dill and season with salt and pepper. Transfer two-thirds of the vegetable mixture to an ovenproof baking dish large enough to hold the fish flat.

Lay the fish on top of the vegetables, then scatter the remaining vegetables on top. Warm the frying pan over medium heat and add the white wine. Bring to a simmer and stir to scrape up any browned bits on the pan bottom. Simmer for 1 minute, and then pour over the fish and vegetables. Cover the dish with foil.

Bake, basting occasionally with the pan juices, until the fish is opaque throughout and an instant-read thermometer inserted into the thickest part of the fish behind the head registers 140°F (60°C), about 30 minutes. Garnish with the dill sprigs and serve directly from the dish.

HALIBUT WITH TOMATOES & LEEKS

Smothering fish fillets in tomatoes and leeks creates an easy, elegant meal in one pan. If desired, cut fresh basil into thin strips (julienne), and use it to garnish the halibut.

serves 4

3 lb (1.5 kg) leeks, white and pale green parts, halved lengthwise and thinly sliced

3 Tbsp olive oil

Salt and freshly ground pepper

2 cups (12 oz/375 g) cherry tomatoes, halved

4 halibut fillets, about 6 oz (185 g) each

Preheat the oven to 450°F (230°C).

In a large roasting pan, toss the leeks with 2 Tbsp of the oil and season with salt and pepper. Spread in a single layer and roast until just tender, about 10 minutes. Remove the pan from the oven and add the tomatoes. Preheat the broiler.

Season the halibut with salt and pepper, and lay the fillets over the leeks and tomatoes. Drizzle with the remaining 1 Tbsp oil. Broil just until the fillets are barely opaque throughout, about 8 minutes. Serve.

In this Vietnamese classic, two seemingly contradictory flavors—intensely sweet caramel and briny fish sauce—reach an enticing harmony by gently simmering together, along with aromatic seasonings. Fish fillets, added during the final minutes of cooking, not only soak up the flavors but also acquire a deep, glossy mahogany color.

VIETNAMESE CLAY POT FISH

serves 6–8

½ cup (4 oz/125 g) sugar

¼ cup (2 fl oz/60 ml) canola oil

3 cloves garlic, minced

3 shallots, minced

1-inch (2.5-cm) piece peeled fresh ginger, grated

2 small red or green Thai chiles or other small hot chiles, halved lengthwise, seeded, and thinly sliced

¼ cup (2 fl oz/60 ml) Asian fish sauce

¼ cup (2 fl oz/60 ml) soy sauce

2 lb (1 kg) firm, mild white fish fillets such as black cod or halibut, cut into equal-sized pieces

Freshly ground pepper

In a small, heavy-bottomed saucepan, combine the sugar and ¼ cup (2 fl oz/60 ml) water. Cook over medium-high heat, stirring occasionally, until the sugar melts. Bring to a boil, stirring frequently, until the mixture turns caramel brown, about 15 minutes. Watch carefully so that it doesn't burn. Remove from the heat and, taking care to avoid splatters, stir in ¼ cup water until thoroughly blended.

In a large, heavy pot, warm the oil over medium-high heat. Add the garlic, shallots, ginger, and chiles and sauté until just tender, 1–2 minutes. Stir in the fish sauce, soy sauce, caramel, and 1 cup (8 fl oz/250 ml) water. Bring to a boil, stirring occasionally.

Reduce the heat to low, partially cover, and cook until the sauce is syrupy but still very fluid, about 15 minutes. If the sauce becomes too thick, stir in ½ cup (4 fl oz/125 ml) water. Add the fish chunks, gently turning to coat with the sauce. Cover and cook, turning the fish once at the midway point, until opaque throughout, about 15 minutes. Season with pepper. Serve the fish in shallow bowls, drizzled with the sauce.

MUSTARD-CRUSTED SALMON WITH RED POTATOES

Spicy mustard rubbed onto fish imparts a quick infusion of flavor. The whole meal goes into the oven at the same time, as waxy new potatoes roast alongside the salmon. Add a salad of peppery arugula or fresh petite peas, and whisk a dollop of mustard into the vinaigrette to bring it all together.

serves 4

1 lb (500 g) red-skinned potatoes, quartered

2 Tbsp olive oil

Salt and freshly ground pepper

¼ cup (2 oz/60 g) Dijon mustard

2 Tbsp dry mustard

4 salmon fillets, about 6 oz (185 g) each, skin removed

4 Tbsp (1 oz/15 g) panko or fresh bread crumbs

¼ cup (½ oz/15 g) chopped fresh flat-leaf parsley

Preheat the oven to 375°F (190°C). In a large roasting pan, toss the potatoes with the olive oil and season with salt and pepper. Spread the potatoes evenly in the pan. Roast until the potatoes are golden, about 10 minutes.

Meanwhile, in a small bowl, stir together the Dijon and dry mustards. Coat one side of the salmon fillets with the mustard mixture, then sprinkle evenly with the panko, gently pressing to adhere.

Arrange the fillets in the pan, breaded side up, next to the potatoes. Bake until the fillets are barely opaque, the topping is golden brown, and the potatoes are tender, 15–18 minutes. Arrange the salmon fillets alongside the potatoes on a platter or individual plates, sprinkle with the parsley, and serve.

SMOKED SALMON FRITTATA WITH GOAT CHEESE & CHIVES

Fold your favorite seasonal ingredients into fluffy eggs for a meal in a skillet. Delicate smoked fish, tangy goat cheese, and fresh, oniony chives evoke spring. Serve with a big bowl of baby greens and a crisp white wine.

serves 8–10

½ lb (250 g) hot-smoked salmon

10 eggs

¼ cup (2 fl oz/60 ml) milk

Salt and freshly ground pepper

4 oz (125 g) fresh goat cheese, crumbled

1 bunch chives, chopped

1 Tbsp olive oil

Preheat the oven to 350°F (180°C). Skin the salmon and break the flesh into bite-sized pieces. In a large bowl, whisk together the eggs, milk, ¼ tsp salt, and ¼ tsp pepper. Gently stir in the salmon, cheese, and chives.

Heat the oil in a 12-inch (30-cm) ovenproof frying pan over medium-high heat. Pour the egg mixture into the pan and reduce the heat to medium. Cook for 1 minute, then transfer to the oven and bake until the frittata is set in the center and slightly puffed up, 25–30 minutes. Let cool in the pan for 5 minutes before serving.

TUNA IN ESCABECHE

serves 4–6

This classic Mediterranean dish pairs meaty fish with a slightly sweet, vinegary sauce and is served cold or at room temperature. Fragrant with orange zest and garlic, it is finished with a sprinkle of chile flakes, just enough spice to give it a bite.

3 Tbsp olive oil

1½ lb (750 g) albacore or yellowfin tuna fillet, about 1 inch (2.5 cm) thick, cut into 6–8 pieces

1 red bell pepper, seeded and thinly sliced

½ red onion, thinly sliced

1 cup (8 fl oz/250 ml) dry white wine

¾ cup (6 fl oz/180 ml) sherry vinegar

2 cloves garlic, crushed

½ tsp black peppercorns

1 tsp grated orange zest

1 tsp sugar

½ tsp red pepper flakes

Salt

½ cup (2½ oz/75 g) pitted olives

In a large frying pan, warm 2 Tbsp of the oil over medium-high heat. Add the tuna and cook, turning once, until browned on both sides but still translucent in the center, 5–8 minutes. Transfer to a 2-qt (2-l) baking dish.

Add the remaining 1 Tbsp olive oil to the pan. Add the bell pepper and onion and sauté until softened, 3–5 minutes. Add the wine, vinegar, garlic, peppercorns, orange zest, sugar, and red pepper flakes. Season with ¾ tsp salt, pour in ¼ cup (2 fl oz/60 ml) water, and bring to a boil.

Pour the hot liquid and vegetables over the fish and scatter the olives over the top. Let stand until cooled to room temperature. Cover and refrigerate for at least 8 hours or up to 24 hours.

Lift the tuna from the marinade and transfer to a platter. Drain the marinade, reserving the vegetables and olives, and arrange them over the tuna. Let stand for about 15 minutes before serving.

GARLICKY SHRIMP SCAMPI

American cooks use the term scampi to describe sautéed jumbo shrimp in a buttery, white wine sauce. Scallops are good with this sauce, too. Small bay scallops will cook in about the same amount of time as the shrimp. If you like, serve the saucy scampi over fresh pasta.

serves 4

½ cup (2½ oz/75 g) all-purpose flour

Salt and freshly ground pepper

2 Tbsp olive oil, plus more as needed

1½ lb (750 g) jumbo or extra-large shrimp, peeled and deveined, tails intact

12 Tbsp (6 oz/185 g) unsalted butter

3 cloves garlic, minced

¼ cup (2 fl oz/60 ml) dry white wine

Grated zest of 1 lemon

2 Tbsp fresh lemon juice

2 Tbsp finely chopped fresh flat-leaf parsley

Lemon wedges

In a shallow bowl, stir together the flour, ½ tsp salt, and ¼ tsp pepper. In a large frying pan, heat the 2 Tbsp oil over medium-high heat. Toss half of the shrimp in the flour mixture to coat evenly, shaking off the excess. Add to the pan and cook, turning occasionally, until opaque throughout, about 3 minutes. Transfer to a plate and tent with foil. Repeat with the remaining shrimp, adding more oil as needed.

Reduce the heat to medium-low, add 2 Tbsp of the butter and the garlic, and cook, stirring frequently, until the garlic softens and is fragrant but not browned, about 2 minutes. Add the wine and the lemon zest and juice and bring to a boil over high heat. Cook until reduced by half, about 1 minute. Reduce the heat to very low. Whisk in the remaining 10 Tbsp butter, 1 Tbsp at a time, letting each addition soften into a creamy emulsion before adding more.

Return the shrimp to the sauce and mix gently to coat well. Remove from the heat and season with salt and pepper. Transfer to a serving dish and sprinkle with the parsley. Serve, passing the lemon wedges at the table.

STIR-FRIED SHRIMP WITH SUGAR SNAP PEAS & MUSHROOMS

serves 4

A Chinese wok is best for stir-frying, but a sauté pan or deep frying pan may also be used. Heat the pan before adding the oil, and swirl to coat the sides as well as the bottom. For best results when stir-frying, have ingredients prepped before you begin, and add quick-cooking foods, such as small pieces of meat, fish, or tofu, separately from slower-cooking foods, such as dense vegetables.

2 lb (1 kg) large shrimp, peeled and deveined

1 tsp toasted sesame oil

1 Tbsp tamari or light soy sauce

Salt

2 Tbsp peanut or canola oil

2 cloves garlic, minced

1 Tbsp peeled and grated fresh ginger

½ lb (250 g) mixed fresh mushrooms, such as oyster or cremini

½ lb (250 g) sugar snap peas, halved crosswise

2 green onions, white and tender green parts, cut into 1-inch (2.5-cm) pieces

2 Tbsp rice wine or dry sherry

Fresh cilantro leaves for garnish

Cooked white rice for serving

In a nonreactive bowl, combine the shrimp, sesame oil, tamari, and 1 tsp salt. Toss to coat.

In a wok or large frying pan, heat the peanut oil over medium-high heat. Add the garlic, ginger, and shrimp and stir-fry until the shrimp are evenly pink on both sides, about 1 minute. Using a slotted spoon, transfer the shrimp to a bowl.

Add the mushrooms to the pan and stir-fry over medium-high heat until they soften, about 3 minutes. Add the sugar snap peas and stir-fry until bright green, about 1 minute. Add the green onions and rice wine. Cover and cook until the snap peas are tender-crisp, about 2 minutes. Return the shrimp to the pan and stir-fry just until heated through, about 1 minute. Garnish with cilantro leaves and serve with the rice.

STIR-FRIED CALAMARI & PEA SHOOTS

Pea shoots are the delicate leaves and tendrils that grow from the vines of the pea plant. Tender and sweet, they are delicious when eaten raw or sautéed. Look for them at the farmers' market in the spring and early summer. Here they are flash-cooked in a hot pan with tender squid rings and tentacles and lots of lemon.

serves 4

4 Tbsp (2 fl oz/60 ml) peanut or canola oil

2 Tbsp minced garlic

1 Tbsp peeled and grated fresh ginger

1 lb (500 g) green pea shoots, tough parts removed

½ cup (1½ oz/45 g) chopped green onions

¼ cup (2 fl oz/60 ml) chicken broth

Salt and freshly ground pepper

1 Tbsp soy sauce

1 tsp chile paste

1 tsp sugar

1 tsp toasted sesame oil

¾ lb (375 g) cleaned squid, cut into bite-size pieces

Cooked rice for serving (optional)

In a wok or large frying pan, heat 2 Tbsp of the peanut oil over medium-high heat. Add the garlic and ginger and stir-fry until fragrant, about 30 seconds. Add the pea shoots and green onions and stir-fry for 3 minutes. Add the broth, ½ tsp salt, and ⅛ tsp pepper and cook until the shoots are tender-crisp, about 2 minutes. Using a slotted spoon, transfer to a plate. Wipe out the pan.

In a small bowl, mix together the soy sauce, chile paste, sugar, and sesame oil.

Warm the remaining 2 Tbsp peanut oil in the pan over medium-high heat. Add the squid and stir-fry until opaque, about 2 minutes. Return the pea shoots to the pan, add the soy sauce mixture, and stir-fry, tossing to combine and heat through, about 1 minute. Using the slotted spoon, transfer the greens and squid to a platter. Serve over rice, if desired.

CALAMARI FRA DIAVOLO

In this classic Italian dish, tender squid rings are smothered with a devilishly spicy tomato sauce. Serve it over a bed of pasta, or pass crusty bread at the table, to help mop up the sauce.

serves 4–6

3 Tbsp olive oil

1 yellow onion, chopped

4 cloves garlic, minced

1 can (28 oz/800 g) whole peeled tomatoes

½ cup (4 fl oz/125 ml) fish broth or bottled clam juice

½ cup (4 fl oz/125 ml) full-bodied red wine

3 Tbsp chopped fresh oregano

½ tsp red pepper flakes

2½ lb (1.25 kg) cleaned squid, bodies cut into ½-inch (12-mm) rings and tentacles coarsely chopped

⅓ cup (½ oz/15 g) chopped fresh flat-leaf parsley

Salt and freshly ground pepper

In a small pot, heat the oil over medium heat. Add the onion and sauté until tender and golden, about 5 minutes. Add the garlic and sauté for 30 seconds. Stir in the tomatoes with their juices, breaking them up with the back of a spoon. Add the broth, wine, 2 Tbsp of the oregano, and the red pepper flakes. Reduce the heat to medium-low and cook, uncovered, until the sauce is lightly thickened and the flavors have blended, 15–20 minutes.

Add the squid, cover, reduce the heat to low, and cook until very tender, 25–30 minutes. Stir in the remaining 1 Tbsp oregano and the parsley. Season with salt and pepper and serve.

PAN-ROASTED CLAMS WITH POTATOES & FENNEL

Nothing could be easier and tastier than this one-pan meal of tender red potatoes, anise-tinged fennel, toasty garlic, and briny littleneck clams. Red pepper flakes and dry white wine finish the dish, mixing with the clams' juices to create a sauce with just a hint of heat.

serves 4

2 lb (1 kg) baby red potatoes, quartered

1 fennel bulb, cut into slices ¼ inch (6 mm) thick, any fronds reserved for garnish

5 cloves garlic, roughly chopped

¼ cup (2 fl oz/60 ml) olive oil

Salt and freshly ground pepper

4 lb (2 kg) littleneck clams, scrubbed and soaked

½ tsp red pepper flakes

¼ cup (2 fl oz/60 ml) dry white wine

Preheat the oven to 475°F (245°C).

Heat a large roasting pan over medium-high heat, add the potatoes, fennel slices, garlic, and oil. Season with 1 tsp salt and ¼ tsp pepper. Cook, stirring, for about 5 minutes. Transfer the pan to the oven and roast until the potatoes have browned, about 20 minutes.

Add the clams, discarding any that do not close to the touch, and the red pepper flakes. Cover the pan and roast, stirring the clams once, until most of the clams have opened, about 15 minutes. Remove the pan from the oven, pour in the wine, cover, and let stand for 1 minute. Discard any unopened clams. Garnish with fennel fronds and serve.

BEEF & VEAL

ITALIAN BRAISED SHORT RIBS

Meaty short ribs go well with the robust flavors of traditional Italian cooking, and slow cooking coaxes them to fall-off-the-bone tenderness. For an extra flourish, garnish each serving with some of the gremolata traditionally sprinkled over Osso Buco (page 76), and serve atop Creamy Polenta (page 33).

serves 6–8

3 Tbsp all-purpose flour

Salt and freshly ground pepper

5½–6 lb (2.75–3 kg) beef short ribs, English cut

¼ cup (2 fl oz/60 ml) olive oil

2 oz (60 g) pancetta, chopped

2 yellow onions, finely chopped

4 cloves garlic, minced

1 tsp red pepper flakes

2 carrots, finely chopped

2 Tbsp tomato paste

1 Tbsp sugar

1 cup (8 fl oz/250 ml) dry red wine

1 can (14½ oz/455 g) diced tomatoes

1 cup (8 fl oz/250 ml) beef broth

¼ cup (2 fl oz/60 ml) balsamic vinegar

2 bay leaves

2 sprigs *each* fresh rosemary and thyme

1 Tbsp dried oregano

On a plate, stir together the flour, 1 tsp salt, and ½ tsp pepper. Turn the ribs in the seasoned flour, shaking off any excess. In a large, heavy pot, heat the oil over medium-high heat. Working in batches, sear the ribs, turning occasionally, until evenly browned, about 10 minutes. Transfer to a plate.

Add the pancetta to the pot and sauté until mostly crisp, 4–5 minutes. Add the onions and sauté until beginning to soften, about 3 minutes. Stir in the garlic and red pepper flakes and sauté until fragrant, about 30 seconds. Add the carrots, tomato paste, and sugar and cook, stirring often, until well blended, about 1 minute. Add the wine, bring to a boil, and stir to scrape up any browned bits on the pan bottom. Stir in the tomatoes and their juices, broth, and vinegar and bring to a boil.

Preheat the oven to 350°F (180°C). Return the ribs to the pot with the tomato mixture. Add the bay leaves, rosemary and thyme sprigs, and oregano. Cover and cook in the oven until the ribs are very tender, about 2 hours.

Skim as much fat as possible from the cooking liquid and discard the bay leaves. Season with salt and pepper and serve.

BEEF BOURGUIGNON

serves 6–8

3½ lb (1.75 kg) boneless beef chuck roast, or a combination of boneless chuck and beef shank, cut into 2–2½ inch (5–6 cm) chunks

Salt and freshly ground pepper

All-purpose flour

1 Tbsp olive oil

6 oz (185 g) pancetta, cut into 1-inch (2.5-cm) pieces

1 carrot, sliced

1 yellow onion, chopped

3 cups (24 fl oz/750 ml) hearty red wine

2 cloves garlic, minced

1 Tbsp fresh thyme leaves, or ½ Tbsp dried thyme

1 bay leaf

1 Tbsp tomato paste

3 Tbsp unsalted butter, plus more if needed

1 lb (500 g) mushrooms, thickly sliced

20–24 jarred or thawed frozen pearl onions

Sprinkle the beef chunks with ½ tsp salt and ¼ tsp pepper. Spread some flour on a large plate. Lightly coat the cubes with the flour, shaking off the excess.

In a large, heavy pot, warm the oil over low heat. Add the pancetta and cook until crisp and golden, 4–5 minutes. Using a slotted spoon, transfer to a large bowl. Raise the heat to medium-high and, working in batches, sear the beef, turning as needed, until browned on all sides, about 5 minutes. Transfer to the bowl with the pancetta. Add the carrot and onion to the pot and cook until browned, about 5 minutes. Transfer to the bowl with the pancetta and beef.

Pour off the fat from the pot. Reduce the heat to medium, add the wine, and stir to scrape up any browned bits on the pot bottom. Stir in the pancetta, beef, carrot, onion, garlic, thyme, bay leaf, and tomato paste. Season with ½ tsp salt and ¼ tsp pepper and bring to a simmer. Reduce the heat to low, cover, and cook until the beef is somewhat tender, about 2½ hours.

In a frying pan, melt the 3 Tbsp butter over medium heat. Add the mushrooms and sauté until lightly browned, 4–5 minutes. Transfer to a bowl. Add the pearl onions to the pan and sauté, adding more butter if needed, until golden, about 10 minutes. After the beef has cooked for 2½ hours, add the mushrooms and pearl onions to the pot and continue to cook until the beef is fork-tender, about 1 hour more.

Transfer the beef, pancetta, and vegetables to a large serving bowl. Skim the fat from the surface of the sauce. Raise the heat to medium- high, bring to a boil, and cook until the sauce thickens slightly, 1–2 minutes. Pour the sauce over the beef mixture and serve.

OSSO BUCO WITH GREMOLATA

serves 6–8

¾ cup (4 oz/125 g) all-purpose flour

Salt and freshly ground pepper

6 bone-in veal shanks, about 6 lb (3 kg) total, each about 1 inch (2.5 cm) thick

½ cup (4 fl oz/120 ml) olive oil

1 yellow onion, chopped

1 carrot, chopped

1 celery rib, chopped

2 cloves garlic, minced

1½ cups (12 fl oz/375 ml) dry red wine

1 cup (6 oz/185 g) canned diced tomatoes

5 cups (40 fl oz/1.25 l) beef broth

FOR THE GREMOLATA

½ cup (¾ oz/20 g) minced fresh flat-leaf parsley

Grated zest of 1 lemon

2 cloves garlic, minced

Put the flour on a plate and season with salt and pepper. Dust the veal shanks with the seasoned flour, shaking off the excess. In a large, heavy sauté pan with a lid, warm the oil over medium-high heat. Working in batches, sear the shanks, turning once, until well browned on both sides, about 8 minutes. Transfer to a plate.

Return the pan to medium heat, add the onion, carrot, celery, and garlic, and sauté until softened, 3–4 minutes. Add the wine and stir to scrape up any browned bits on the pan bottom. Raise the heat to high and cook until the liquid has thickened and is reduced by half, 3–4 minutes. Add the tomatoes and broth and bring to a boil. Reduce the heat to low, return the veal shanks to the pan, cover, and simmer, turning occasionally, for 1 hour. Uncover and cook until the veal is tender, about 30 minutes.

Meanwhile, to make the gremolata, in a small bowl, stir together the parsley, lemon zest, and garlic.

Divide the veal shanks among plates. Top with the pan sauce, sprinkle with the gremolata, and serve.

Most Lone Star chili masters eschew beans and tomatoes. To them, chili is all about the meat—beef only—and the seasoning. Purists also claim that toppings turn their bowl of red into a salad bar. But you can opt for anything you like, such as sour cream, shredded cheese, red onions—even a handful of tortilla chips for crunch.

TEXAS BEEF CHILI

serves 8

2 tsp cumin seeds, toasted

¼ cup (¾ oz/20 g) pure ancho chile powder

1 Tbsp Spanish smoked paprika

2 tsp dried oregano

4 lb (2 kg) boneless beef chuck roast, cut into ½-inch (12-mm) chunks

Salt and freshly ground pepper

3 Tbsp olive oil

1 large yellow onion, chopped

1 jalapeño chile, seeded and minced

1 large red bell pepper, seeded and chopped

4 cloves garlic, minced

1½ cups (12 fl oz/375 ml) lager beer

1 cup (8 fl oz/250 ml) beef broth

2 Tbsp yellow cornmeal

Shredded Cheddar cheese, chopped red onions, sour cream, and minced jalapeño chiles for serving (optional)

Using a mortar and pestle or a spice grinder, finely grind the cumin seeds. Transfer to a bowl, add the chile powder, paprika, and oregano, and mix well. Set aside.

Season the beef with salt and pepper. In a large, heavy pot, heat 2 Tbsp of the oil over medium-high heat. Working in batches, sear the beef, turning occasionally, until browned, about 5 minutes. Transfer to a plate.

Add the remaining 1 Tbsp oil to the pot. Add the onion, jalapeño, bell pepper, and garlic and reduce the heat to medium. Cover and cook, stirring occasionally, until the onion softens, about 5 minutes. Uncover, add the spice mixture, and stir well for 30 seconds. Stir in the beer and broth. Return the beef to the pot, cover, and reduce the heat to low. Simmer until the beef is fork-tender, 1½–2 hours.

Remove the chili from the heat and let stand for 5 minutes. Skim any fat from the surface. Bring the chili to a simmer over medium heat. Transfer about ½ cup (4 fl oz/125 ml) of the cooking liquid to a small bowl and whisk in the cornmeal. Stir into the chili and cook until lightly thickened, about 1 minute. Season with salt and pepper. Spoon the chili into bowls and serve, garnished with cheese, red onions, sour cream, or jalapeños, if you like.

BEEF WITH MUSHROOMS & BARLEY

Tender chunks of stewed beef, meaty mushrooms, and pleasantly chewy grains create a bowl brimming with texture and flavor. Look to any varieties of wild mushrooms that are still in season, before they vanish with the spring showers.

serves 4–6

1 oz (30 g) dried mushrooms, such as porcini

2 cups (16 fl oz/500 ml) boiling water

2 Tbsp unsalted butter

2 lb (1 kg) beef chuck, cut into 2-inch (5-cm) pieces

2 yellow onions, finely chopped

2 cloves garlic, minced

1 lb (500 g) small cremini or other fresh mushrooms, trimmed

2 cups (16 fl oz/500 ml) beef broth

½ cup (4 oz/125 g) pearl barley

3 carrots, finely chopped

2 parsnips, peeled and finely chopped

Salt and freshly ground pepper

2 Tbsp chopped fresh dill

Put the dried mushrooms in a bowl, add the boiling water, and soak for 20 minutes. Line a fine-mesh sieve with a double layer of cheesecloth, place over a bowl, and drain the mushrooms, reserving the soaking liquid. Rinse the mushrooms with cold water and chop finely.

Preheat the oven to 300°F (150°C). In a large, heavy pot, melt the butter over medium-high heat. Working in batches, sear the beef in the butter, turning frequently, until browned on all sides, about 10 minutes. Transfer to a plate.

Add the onions and garlic and sauté until softened, 5–7 minutes. Stir in the rehydrated mushrooms. Add the fresh mushrooms, reduce the heat to medium, and sauté until they start to brown and release their liquid, about 5 minutes. Stir in the mushroom soaking liquid and the broth. Return the beef to the pot and stir to combine. Cover and cook in the oven until the beef is tender, about 2 hours.

Stir in the barley and 1 cup (8 fl oz/250 ml) water and cook, covered, for 1 hour. Stir in the carrots and parsnips and cook, covered, until the barley and vegetables are tender, about 30 minutes. Season with salt and pepper. Garnish with the dill and serve.

BEEF & BASIL STIR-FRY WITH SUMMER VEGETABLES

Thai basil, with its beautiful purple stems, adds an incredible flavor and aroma to this dish. But if you can't find Thai basil, you can substitute sweet basil. This stir-fry is wonderful on its own or served over steamed rice or fresh Asian noodles.

serves 4

¼ cup (2 fl oz/60 ml) soy sauce

3 Tbsp sherry

1 Tbsp honey

1 tsp cornstarch

2 Tbsp canola oil

1 lb (500 g) flank steak, thinly sliced, then cut into 1-inch (2.5-cm) pieces

Salt and freshly ground pepper

2 cloves garlic, minced

1-inch (2.5-cm) piece peeled fresh ginger, grated

1 yellow squash, cut into ½-inch (12-mm) matchsticks

2 carrots, cut into ½-inch (12-mm) matchsticks

4 oz (125 g) sugar snap peas, trimmed and halved

¼ cup (¼ oz/7 g) small fresh basil leaves, preferably Thai

In a small bowl, stir together the soy sauce, sherry, honey, and cornstarch.

In a wok or large frying pan, heat 1 Tbsp of the oil over high heat. Season the steak pieces with salt and pepper. Add to the pan and, tossing to sear on all sides, cook until browned but still rare inside, about 3 minutes. Transfer to a plate. Pour off any fat from the pan.

Return the pan to high heat and warm the remaining 1 Tbsp oil. Add the garlic and ginger and stir-fry until fragrant, about 1 minute, taking care not to let the garlic and ginger brown. Add the squash, carrots, and sugar snap peas and stir-fry for 4 minutes. Add the steak and the soy sauce mixture and stir to combine. Cook, stirring often, until the sauce thickens, about 3 minutes. Top with the basil leaves and serve.

STIR-FRIED TRI-TIP WITH RADICCHIO

Although tri-tip is often grilled, its leanness makes it a better candidate for stir-frying. When stir-fried, the meat can absorb the flavors of the other ingredients, rather than drying out from the heat of the grill. Pleasantly bitter radicchio crisps in the same pan, and peppery watercress provides a refreshing accent.

serves 4

1 tri-tip roast or top sirloin steak, about 1 lb (500 g)

1 large head radicchio, 8–9 oz (250–280 g)

Salt and freshly ground pepper

2 Tbsp olive oil

2 Tbsp unsalted butter

1 large shallot, minced

1 small bunch watercress, tough stems removed

1 tsp white or red wine vinegar

Put the beef in the freezer for 20 minutes to firm it up for slicing thin. Meanwhile, core the radicchio and cut lengthwise into quarters. Cut each quarter crosswise into thin slivers.

Cut the partially frozen beef in half lengthwise, then cut each half across the grain into slices about ¼ inch (6 mm) thick. Season the slices generously with salt and pepper.

In a large wok or frying pan, heat 1 Tbsp of the oil over medium-high heat. Add half of the beef, distributing it evenly, and cook without moving it for about 20 seconds. Continue to cook the beef, tossing and stirring it every 15–20 seconds, until browned but still slightly pink inside, 2–3 minutes. Transfer to a platter. Repeat to cook the remaining beef in the remaining 1 Tbsp oil, and transfer to the platter with the first batch.

Pour off most of the oil from the pan. Reduce the heat to medium and add the butter. Add the radicchio and shallot, and stir-fry until the radicchio is wilted and tender, 3–4 minutes. Season with salt and pepper. Return the beef and any juices to the pan. Add the watercress and vinegar. Stir-fry for about 1 minute to warm the beef and wilt the watercress, then serve.

STEAK PIPERADE

Piperade, a basque-style mixture of sweet peppers and onions, is an excellent topping for quick-cooking steaks. Searing the steaks in a pan leaves some meaty flavor for the peppers, but you could also fire up the grill.

serves 4

1½ lb (750 g) skirt or flank steak

Salt and freshly ground pepper

2 Tbsp unsalted butter

2 Tbsp olive oil

1 red onion, chopped

3 red or yellow bell peppers, seeded and thinly sliced crosswise

3 cloves garlic, minced

1 Tbsp chopped fresh thyme

½ cup (4 fl oz/125 ml) dry white wine

1 can (14½ oz/455 g) diced tomatoes

Season the steak generously with salt and pepper. In a large frying pan, melt 1 Tbsp of the butter with 1 Tbsp of the oil over high heat. Add the steak and cook, turning once, for 4–6 minutes for medium-rare, or until done to your liking. Transfer the meat to a carving board and tent with foil.

Melt the remaining 1 Tbsp butter with the remaining 1 Tbsp oil in the same pan over medium heat. Add the onion, bell peppers, garlic, and thyme and sauté until the onion is barely softened, 3–4 minutes. Add the wine, bring to a boil, stir to scrape up any browned bits on the pan bottom, and cook for about 30 seconds. Stir in the tomatoes and their juice and simmer until the liquid is slightly reduced, about 5 minutes. Season with salt and pepper.

Cut the meat thinly across the grain on the diagonal. Arrange the slices on a warm platter, spoon the pepper sauce over the slices, and serve.

Brisket is one of the glories of grilling season, but even if you own a smoker it can be a labor of love. Slow cooking it in the oven produces equally tender results, and is much easier. Beef brisket is sold without the bone and is divided into two sections, the flat cut and the point cut. At the meat counter, ask for the flat cut if possible. It has less fat and is easier to slice.

BARBECUE-STYLE BRISKET

serves 6–8

¼ cup (2 oz/60 g) firmly packed dark brown sugar

¼ cup (2 fl oz/60 ml) cider vinegar

2 tomatoes, seeded and chopped

2 cups (16 fl oz/500 ml) beef broth

3 lb (1.5 kg) beef brisket

Salt and freshly ground pepper

2 Tbsp canola oil

2 yellow onions, thinly sliced

2 cloves garlic, minced

½ tsp ground allspice

2 Tbsp all-purpose flour

In a small bowl, stir together the sugar, vinegar, tomatoes, and broth. Set aside.

Season the brisket generously with salt and pepper. In a large, heavy pot, heat the oil over medium-high heat. Add the brisket, fat side down, and cook, turning once, until browned on both sides, about 10 minutes. Transfer to a plate.

Pour off all but 2 Tbsp of the fat from the pot. Add the onions and sauté over medium-high heat until softened, about 3 minutes. Add the garlic and sauté for 1 minute. Stir in the allspice. Sprinkle the flour over the onion mixture, reduce the heat to medium, and cook, stirring frequently, until blended, about 3 minutes. Pour in the reserved broth mixture and stir to combine. Bring to a boil and season with salt and pepper.

Preheat the oven to 300°F (150°C). Return the brisket to the pot, cover, and cook in the oven until the brisket is very tender, 3–4 hours. Skim the fat from the surface of the cooking liquid.

Let the brisket cool in the cooking liquid then transfer the brisket to a cutting board and slice the brisket across the grain. Warm the cooking liquid over medium heat. Arrange the slices on a platter, top with the warm cooking liquid and onions, and serve.

Winter produces the crispest, crunchiest cabbages of the year, and bok choy is no exception. Pair it with thinly sliced flank steak, and season with a few simple but bold seasonings. Serve this quick and hearty stir-fry with wide rice noodles or steamed brown rice, if you like.

STIR-FRIED BEEF & BOK CHOY WITH GINGER

serves 4

2 Tbsp dry sherry

1 Tbsp soy sauce

½ tsp Asian chile paste

1 lb (500 g) baby bok choy

2 tsp peanut oil

2 cloves garlic, minced

1 Tbsp peeled and grated fresh ginger

1 lb (500 g) flank steak, thinly sliced across the grain

In a small bowl, stir together the sherry, soy sauce, and chile paste. Cut the bok choy lengthwise into halves or quarters, depending on size.

In a wok or a large frying pan, heat 1½ tsp of the oil over high heat. Add the bok choy and stir-fry just until tender-crisp, 3–4 minutes. Transfer to a bowl.

Add the remaining ½ tsp oil to the pan. Add the garlic and ginger and stir-fry until fragrant but not browned, 15–30 seconds. Add the beef and cook, stirring, just until no longer pink, about 2 minutes.

Return the bok choy to the pan, add the sherry mixture, and cook for 1 minute until heated through. Serve.

STIR-FRIED SOBA NOODLES WITH BEEF & CABBAGE

serves 4

1 lb (500 g) boneless beef sirloin or tenderloin, partially frozen

¼ cup (2 fl oz/60 ml) toasted sesame oil

¼ cup (2 fl oz/60 ml) soy sauce

¼ cup (2 fl oz/60 ml) plus 1 Tbsp peanut oil

2 Tbsp peeled and grated fresh ginger

Salt

¾ lb (375 g) dried soba noodles

2 large cloves garlic, minced

4 green onions, including 3 inches (7.5 cm) of green tops, thinly sliced on the diagonal

1 head napa cabbage, about 2 lb (1 kg), cored and shredded

2 cups (16 fl oz/500 ml) chicken or beef broth

1 Tbsp cornstarch

½ lb (250 g) snow peas, trimmed and halved crosswise

¼ cup (1 oz/30 g) sesame seeds, lightly toasted

Using a sharp knife, cut the beef across the grain into thin slices, then cut the slices into matchsticks. In a bowl, whisk together the sesame oil, soy sauce, ¼ cup peanut oil, and ginger. Add the beef and stir to coat evenly. Cover and refrigerate, stirring occasionally, for at least 1 hour or up to 3 hours.

Bring a large pot of water to a rapid boil. Add 2 Tbsp salt and the noodles to the boiling water, stir well, and cook, stirring occasionally, until just tender, 5–7 minutes. Drain the noodles.

Meanwhile, in a wok or large frying pan, heat the 1 Tbsp peanut oil over medium-high heat. Add the garlic and green onions and stir-fry until lightly colored, about 1 minute. Raise the heat to high, add the beef and its marinade, and stir-fry until lightly browned, about 8 minutes. Add the cabbage and 1½ cups (12 fl oz/375 ml) of the broth and toss to combine. Cover, reduce the heat to medium-high, and cook until the cabbage wilts, about 4 minutes.

In a small bowl, whisk the cornstarch into the remaining ½ cup (4 fl oz/125 ml) broth. Add the cornstarch mixture to the pan, and stir and toss to incorporate. Add the snow peas, stir and toss to combine, cover, and cook until just tender, about 2 minutes. Take care not to overcook; the snow peas and cabbage should remain crisp.

Add the noodles to the pan and stir and toss until well combined. Garnish with the toasted sesame seeds, and serve.

BEEF, BASIL & GOAT CHEESE LASAGNA ROLL-UPS

Tidy bundles of pasta and filling are easy to dish out to family and friends. Four different cheeses verges on indulgent, but the goat cheese is essential, adding unique flavor and creamy texture. Save any extra meat filling for another use, or simply tuck it in around the rolls. A big green salad, garlic bread, and a dry red wine complete this dinner.

serves 6–8

3 Tbsp olive oil

1 yellow onion, chopped

3 cloves garlic, minced

¼ tsp red pepper flakes (optional)

Salt and freshly ground pepper

1 can (28 oz/875 g) crushed tomatoes

¾ lb (375 g) dried lasagna noodles

1 lb (500 g) ground beef

½ lb (250 g) ricotta cheese

4 oz (125 g) fresh goat cheese

1 cup (4 oz/125 g) grated Parmesan cheese

1 egg, lightly beaten

⅓ cup (½ oz/15 g) chopped fresh basil

1 cup (4 oz/125 g) shredded mozzarella cheese

In a large saucepan, warm 2 Tbsp oil over medium-high heat. Add the onion and sauté until it begins to soften, about 4 minutes. Stir in the garlic, the red pepper flakes (if using), 2 tsp salt, and 1 tsp pepper and cook for 2 minutes. Add the tomatoes and stir to combine. Bring the sauce to a boil, reduce the heat to low, and simmer to allow the flavors to develop, about 20 minutes. Season again with salt and pepper.

Bring a large pot of salted water to a boil. Add the lasagna noodles and cook until al dente, according to the package directions. Drain the noodles and arrange in a single layer on a baking sheet.

Preheat the oven to 400°F (200°C).

In a frying pan, warm the remaining 1 Tbsp oil over medium-high heat. Add the ground beef and cook, stirring to break it up into small pieces, until browned, about 6 minutes. Season with salt and pepper, transfer to a large bowl, and let cool slightly. Add the ricotta, the goat cheese, half of the Parmesan, the egg, the basil, and ⅓ cup (3 fl oz/80 ml) of the tomato sauce and stir to combine.

Ladle 1½ cups (12 fl oz/375 ml) of the tomato sauce into the bottom of a 9-by-13-inch (23-by-33-cm) baking dish. Lay a noodle on a work surface. Put ⅓ cup of the meat mixture on one end and roll up the noodle. Place the roll, seam side down, in the dish. Repeat with the remaining noodles and meat mixture. Cover the roll-ups with the remaining tomato sauce. Sprinkle with the mozzarella and the remaining Parmesan.

Bake until the sauce is bubbling and the cheese is melted, about 20 minutes. Serve.

MEATBALLS IN TOMATO SAUCE

Using a trio of meats is perfect for these tender meatballs. Beef adds hearty flavor, while pork and veal provide a natural sweetness. It is best to use an equal amount of each for the perfect blend. Unlike most recipes that call for browning the meatballs, this one braises them in an herbed tomato sauce. The meatballs and sauce can be prepared a day ahead, refrigerated, and reheated before serving.

serves 4

FOR THE MEATBALLS

2 lb (1 kg) mixed ground beef, pork, and veal

1 egg

1 small yellow onion, finely chopped

½ cup (1 oz/30 g) fresh bread crumbs or panko

¼ cup (1 oz/30 g) pine nuts, toasted

¼ cup (1 oz/30 g) grated Parmesan or Romano cheese

2 Tbsp chopped fresh flat-leaf parsley

1 Tbsp chopped fresh oregano

1 Tbsp chopped fresh basil

Salt and freshly ground pepper

2 Tbsp olive oil

1 yellow onion, chopped

3 cloves garlic, minced

1 can (28 oz/875 g) diced tomatoes with juice

½ cup (4 fl oz/125 ml) dry white wine

2 Tbsp chopped fresh basil (optional)

To make the meatballs, in a large bowl, combine the ground meats, egg, the finely chopped onion, bread crumbs, pine nuts, Parmesan, parsley, oregano, and basil. Season with ¾ tsp salt and ½ tsp pepper. Using your hands, gently but thoroughly blend the ingredients. Form the mixture into meatballs about 2 inches (5 cm) in diameter.

To make the sauce, in a large, heavy saucepan, heat the oil over medium heat. Add the chopped onion and sauté until softened, 4–5 minutes. Add the garlic and sauté for 30 seconds. Stir in the tomatoes and wine and bring to a boil. Lower the meatballs into the sauce, gently spooning the sauce over them. Bring to a simmer, reduce the heat to medium-low, cover, and cook until the meatballs are firm and cooked through, 20–30 minutes.

Remove from the heat and let stand for 5 minutes. Stir in the basil (if using). Transfer the meatballs and tomato sauce to a large shallow bowl and serve.

PORK

Traditional cassoulet is a hearty, rustic dish, combining several types of meat with beans. Most busy home cooks don't have time to slowly poach a duck confit, but you can try this approximation instead. It takes a few well-advised shortcuts with quality pork sausages, bacon, and canned beans.

QUICK CASSOULET

serves 4–6

1½ lb (750 g) pork sausages

2 Tbsp olive oil, plus more as needed

5 slices thick-cut bacon, chopped

1 yellow onion, chopped

4 cloves garlic

4 cans (15 oz/470 g each) cannellini or navy beans, rinsed and drained

1 cup (8 fl oz/250 ml) chicken broth

1 sprig fresh thyme

1 can (14½ oz/455 g) diced tomatoes

1½ tsp sugar

Salt and freshly ground pepper

1 cup (2 oz/60 g) fresh bread crumbs (optional)

4 Tbsp (2 oz/60 g) unsalted butter, melted (optional)

Slit each sausage diagonally several times on each side. In a large frying pan, warm 1 Tbsp of the oil over medium heat. Add the sausages and cook, turning once, until browned on the outside and cooked through, about 10 minutes. Transfer to a plate.

Add the remaining 1 Tbsp oil to the frying pan, add the bacon, and sauté until it starts to brown, about 5 minutes. Transfer to a plate.

Drain off all but 2 Tbsp fat from the pan, adding some olive oil if necessary. Increase the heat to medium-high and add the onion and garlic to the pan. Sauté until the onion is translucent, about 4 minutes. Add the beans and broth and bring to a simmer. Reduce the heat to medium-low and simmer to blend the flavors, about 15 minutes. Stir in the bacon, thyme, tomatoes, and sugar. Bring to a simmer and cook, stirring frequently, until the flavors are blended, about 5 minutes. Season with salt and pepper.

Grease a 3-qt (3-l) baking dish and distribute the sausages evenly in the dish. Spoon the bean mixture over the sausages. If desired, spread the bread crumbs on top and drizzle with the melted butter. Bake until the beans are bubbly and the crumb topping is golden brown, about 20 minutes. Let cool slightly before serving.

BEER-BRAISED PORK ROAST

serves 4–6

In this recipe the pleasant flavor of beer permeates the pork during slow cooking. The butt, used here, is the top end of a whole leg of the pig. The shoulder, although a little fattier and with more connective tissue, makes a good alternative for beer-braising. Serve with buttered egg noodles or polenta.

1 pork butt roast, about 4 lb (2 kg), trimmed

Salt and freshly ground pepper

2 Tbsp canola oil

2 yellow onions, thinly sliced

1 carrot, chopped

2 cloves garlic, minced

1 Tbsp tomato paste

3 Tbsp all-purpose flour

1 bottle (12 fl oz/375 ml) dark beer or ale

½ cup (4 fl oz/125 ml) apple cider

1 cup (8 fl oz/250 ml) chicken broth

1 Tbsp apple cider vinegar

5–6 sprigs fresh thyme

Season the pork generously with salt and pepper. In a large, heavy pot, heat the oil over medium-high heat. Add the pork and cook, turning occasionally, until browned on all sides, about 10 minutes total. Transfer to a plate.

Preheat the oven to 300°F (150°C). Pour off all but 1 Tbsp fat from the pot. Add the onions, carrot, and garlic and sauté over medium-high heat until softened, about 5 minutes. Stir in the tomato paste and cook, stirring frequently, until the mixture starts to become dry, about 2 minutes. Add the flour and cook, stirring constantly, for 2 minutes. Pour in the beer and stir to scrape up any browned bits on the pot bottom. Cook until the liquid starts to thicken, about 10 minutes. Stir in the cider, broth, vinegar, and thyme. Season with salt and pepper and bring to a boil.

Return the pork to the pot, cover, and cook in the oven for about 3 hours. Uncover and continue to cook, basting frequently with the braising liquid, until the pork is tender, about 1 hour longer.

Transfer the pork to a cutting board and cover loosely with foil. Skim the excess fat from the surface of the cooking liquid. Cut the pork across the grain into thin slices. Arrange the slices on a platter, spoon the cooking juices over the top and serve.

GARLICKY PORK SHOULDER WITH GREENS

Pork shoulder is a beautifully marbled cut, which emerges fork-tender after a long cooking at low temperatures. Rub down the meat with woodsy rosemary and pungent garlic for a boldly flavored, satisfying stew.

serves 6

2½ lb (1.25 kg) boneless pork shoulder, cut into 1½-inch (4-cm) chunks

Salt and freshly ground pepper

2 Tbsp olive oil

1 large yellow onion, finely chopped

2 sprigs fresh thyme

15–20 cloves garlic

1 tsp minced fresh rosemary

⅔ cup (5 fl oz/160 ml) dry red wine

1 Tbsp red wine vinegar

⅔ cup (5 fl oz/160 ml) beef or chicken broth

About 1¼ lb (625 g) kale, tough stems removed, leaves cut crosswise into wide strips

Season the pork generously with salt and pepper. In a large frying pan, heat the oil over medium-high heat. Working in batches, add the pork and sear, turning as needed, until well browned on all sides, 6–7 minutes. Using a slotted spoon, transfer to a plate.

Pour off most of the fat from the pan and return to medium-high heat. Add the onion and thyme and sauté until the onion is golden brown, about 5 minutes. Add the garlic and rosemary and cook for 1 minute. Pour in the wine and vinegar and stir to scrape up any browned bits on the pan bottom. Transfer the contents of the pan to a slow cooker. Add the broth and the pork and stir to combine. Cover and cook on the low setting for 5–6 hours, stirring two or three times during the first 2 hours. Stir in the kale, re-cover, and cook for 30–60 minutes. The pork and kale should be very tender.

Using the slotted spoon, transfer the pork and kale to a platter. Skim any fat from the cooking liquid, then drizzle the liquid over the meat and serve.

PORK MEDALLIONS WITH ROASTED NECTARINES

Lean pork tenderloin cooks quickly when sliced across the grain into neat rounds. Match the inherent sweetness of the meat with juicy, late-summer nectarines, which caramelize in the heat of the pan. This recipe would also be delicious with peaches or in autumn with fresh figs.

serves 4

1 pork tenderloin, about 1½ lb (750 g), cut crosswise into 4–6 medallions

Salt and freshly ground pepper

1 Tbsp olive oil

1 cup (8 fl oz/250 ml) hard apple cider

1 sprig fresh rosemary

2 tsp grainy mustard

2 nectarines or peaches, halved, pitted, and cut into wedges, or 6 figs, halved lengthwise

1 Tbsp unsalted butter

Preheat the oven to 400°F (200°C).

Season the pork with salt and pepper. In an ovenproof frying pan, heat the oil over medium-high heat. Add the pork medallions and cook, turning once, until browned, 4–5 minutes. Transfer to a plate.

Add the cider, rosemary, and mustard to the pan, bring to a boil, and stir to scrape up any browned bits on the pan bottom. Cook until the liquid is reduced by half, 3–4 minutes. Return the pork to the pan, place in the oven, and cook for about 6 minutes. Remove from the oven, turn the pork, and add the sliced nectarines. Return to the oven and cook until the pork is tender and registers 145°F (63°C) on an instant-read thermometer, 6–8 minutes.

Transfer the pork and nectarines to a platter. Place the pan over medium heat and whisk in the butter to make a sauce. Spoon the sauce over the pork and nectarines and serve.

SPICY PORK & EGGPLANT STIR-FRY

Here, cubes of deeply purple eggplant are tossed with tender pieces of pork in a fiery chile sauce. The eggplant flesh emerges from the wok seared on the outside but silken at heart.

serves 4

1 pork tenderloin, about 1 lb (500 g), silverskin removed

Salt and freshly ground pepper

1 eggplant, about 1 lb (500 g)

2 Tbsp chile-garlic sauce, such as Sriracha

1½ tsp toasted sesame oil

1½ tsp rice vinegar

3 Tbsp peanut or canola oil

1 Tbsp peeled and grated fresh ginger

6 green onions, white and tender green parts, 4 halved lengthwise and cut into ¾-inch (2-cm) pieces, 2 finely chopped

Put the pork in the freezer for 20 minutes to firm it up for slicing. Cut into strips about ½ inch (12 mm) thick, 2 inches (5 cm) long, and ¾ inch (2 cm) wide. Season generously with salt and pepper. Cut the eggplant into strips of the same size.

In a small bowl, whisk together the chile-garlic sauce, sesame oil, and vinegar until smooth. Set aside.

In a wok or large frying pan, heat 2 Tbsp of the peanut oil over high heat until very hot. Add the eggplant and stir-fry until slightly softened, 3–4 minutes. Add the ginger and the green onion pieces and stir-fry for 1 minute. Transfer the vegetables to a platter.

Add the remaining 1 Tbsp peanut oil to the pan over high heat and swirl to coat. Add the pork, distributing it evenly, and cook without moving it for about 20 seconds. With a metal spatula, toss and stir the pork every 15–20 seconds until browned, about 3 minutes. Return the vegetables to the pan and add the chile-garlic mixture. Reduce the heat to medium and stir-fry for 1–2 minutes to blend the flavors and warm through. Scatter with the chopped green onions and serve.

BRAISED PORK CHOPS WITH CHERRIES

Cherries pair well with duck or pork in savory dishes, bringing out the natural sweetness of the meat. A cherry pitter will make short work of the stones. When fresh cherries aren't in season, use dried cherries.

serves 4

4 bone-in, center-cut pork loin chops, each 1 inch (2.5 cm) thick

Salt and freshly ground pepper

1 Tbsp minced fresh rosemary

3 Tbsp unsalted butter

2 leeks, white and pale green parts, halved lengthwise and thinly sliced

1 cup (8 fl oz/250 ml) chicken broth

¼ cup (2 fl oz/60 ml) Port wine

2 Tbsp balsamic vinegar

½ cup (2 oz/60 g) dried cherries or 1 cup (4 oz/120 g) fresh pitted cherries, halved

Season the pork chops with salt and pepper and sprinkle with the rosemary, patting the seasonings firmly to adhere to the meat. In a sauté pan with a lid, melt 2 Tbsp of the butter over medium-high heat. Add the pork chops and cook, turning once, until golden on both sides, about 6 minutes. Transfer to a plate.

In the same pan, melt the remaining 1 Tbsp butter over medium heat. Add the leeks and sauté until softened and beginning to brown, 3–4 minutes. Stir in the broth, stir to scrape up any browned bits on the pan bottom, and cook for 1 minute. Stir in the wine, vinegar, and cherries.

Return the pork chops and any juices to the pan and spoon the liquid over them. Cover, reduce the heat to medium-low, and simmer until the pork is tender and barely pink in the center, about 15 minutes. Divide the chops among plates, spoon the cherry mixture over the top, and serve.

PULLED PORK WITH SPICY PEACH-MUSTARD SAUCE

This pulled pork, doused in a sweet-and-sour soaking sauce with a generous helping of peach jam, is perfect picnic fare. Serve it on a platter alongside soft sandwich rolls, sliced dill pickles, and coleslaw, allowing diners to assemble their own sandwiches.

serves 12

Oil for pan

1 bone-in pork shoulder, about 6 lb (3 kg)

Salt and freshly ground pepper

1 Tbsp mustard seeds

2 cups (16 fl oz/500 ml) cider vinegar

4 yellow onions, sliced, plus 3 onions, chopped

½ cup (4 oz/125 g) unsalted butter

3 cloves garlic, minced

2 cups (16 fl oz/500 ml) canned crushed tomatoes

2 Tbsp tomato paste

1 cup (10 oz/315 g) peach jam

½ cup (4 oz/125 g) Dijon mustard

½ cup (4 fl oz/125 ml) aged Kentucky bourbon

½ cup (6 oz/185 g) honey

¼ cup (2 oz/60 g) firmly packed dark brown sugar

1 Tbsp hot-pepper sauce

12 soft sandwich rolls

Preheat the oven to 300°F (150°C). Lightly oil a large roasting pan.

Put the pork shoulder in the prepared pan and rub with 1 Tbsp salt, 1 Tbsp pepper, and the mustard seeds. Pour 1 cup (8 fl oz/250 ml) of the vinegar and 1 cup (8 fl oz/250 ml) water over and around the pork. Scatter the sliced onions over and around the meat. Cover with foil and roast for 4 hours.

Meanwhile, in a saucepan, melt the butter over medium heat. Add the chopped onions and the garlic and cook, stirring occasionally, until the onions are soft and beginning to brown, about 10 minutes. Add the tomatoes, tomato paste, jam, mustard, bourbon, honey, brown sugar, remaining 1 cup vinegar, and hot-pepper sauce and stir to mix well. Season with salt and pepper. Bring to a boil, reduce the heat to very low, and simmer, uncovered, stirring occasionally, until the sauce is dark and thick, about 2 hours. Let cool for 15 minutes.

Remove the foil and continue to roast until an instant-read thermometer inserted into the thickest part of the pork away from the bone registers 180°F (82°C) and the juices run clear, about 1 hour. Remove the pork from the pan and let stand for 1 hour. Using 2 forks, shred the pork, discarding any fat. Put the pork in a bowl. Using a slotted spoon, lift the roasted onions from the pan and add to the pork. Mix well to combine.

Mix half of the sauce with the shredded pork. Mound the pork on a large platter and place the rolls on a plate. Serve, passing the remaining sauce at the table.

CIDER-BRAISED PORK CHOPS WITH APPLES

While Fuji apples are a good choice here, pair any crisp, slightly tart apple that's in season at your local farmers' market. Braising the spice-coated pork chops in cider enhances the autumnal flavor.

serves 4

1 tsp dried oregano

½ tsp five-spice powder

½ tsp sweet paprika

Salt and freshly ground pepper

4 thin boneless center-cut pork loin chops, about 1 lb (500 g) total

4 tsp canola oil

1 yellow onion, thinly sliced

⅓ cup (3 fl oz/80 ml) apple cider

2 Tbsp red wine vinegar

1 Fuji apple, peeled, halved, cored, and cut into 8 wedges

1 cup (8 fl oz/250 ml) chicken broth

¼ cup (2 fl oz/60 ml) evaporated milk

In a small bowl, stir together the oregano, five-spice powder, paprika, ½ tsp salt, and ¼ tsp pepper. Coat the pork chops evenly on both sides with the spice mixture. Set the meat on a plate and let stand for 10 minutes.

In a large, deep frying pan, warm 2 tsp of the oil over medium-high heat. Add the onion and sauté until lightly browned, about 5 minutes. Transfer to a plate.

Add the remaining 2 tsp oil to the pan and return it to medium-high heat. Add the pork chops and sear until lightly browned, about 4 minutes. Turn and brown on the second side, 3–4 minutes. Transfer to the plate holding the onion.

Place the pan over medium heat and pour in the cider and vinegar. Stir to scrape up any browned bits on the pan bottom. Return the pork and onion to the pan and arrange the apple wedges on top of the pork. Pour in the broth, cover, and simmer until the chops are opaque throughout, about 10 minutes, reducing the heat if the liquid begins to boil.

Transfer the chops, apple wedges, and onion to a platter. Pour the milk into the pan, raise the heat to high, and boil until the liquid is reduced by one-third, about 5 minutes. Pour the sauce over the chops and serve.

Warm up on cold days with spicy Latin flavors. Chorizo sausage puts a kick into this stew, which is extra satisfying due to the double dose of protein from beans and the meat.

SPICY RED BEAN & CHORIZO STEW

serves 6–8

2¼ cups (1 lb/500 g) dried red kidney beans, picked over and rinsed

2 Tbsp canola oil

1 large yellow onion, finely chopped

3 celery ribs, finely chopped

1 green bell pepper, seeded and chopped

6 cloves garlic, minced

Salt and freshly ground pepper

4 cups (32 fl oz/1 l) beef or chicken broth

2 tsp red wine vinegar

½–¾ tsp red pepper flakes

3 bay leaves

1 lb (500 g) cured Spanish-style chorizo, cut into slices ¼ inch (6 mm) thick

Hot-pepper sauce, such as Tabasco

Cooked white rice for serving

Place the beans in a large bowl with cold water to cover and soak for at least 4 hours or up to overnight. (For a quick soak, combine the beans and water to cover in a large pot, bring to a boil, remove from the heat, cover, and soak for 1 hour.) Drain and rinse the beans.

In a large, heavy frying pan, heat the oil over medium-high heat. Add the onion, celery, and bell pepper and sauté until softened and just beginning to brown, about 6 minutes. Add the garlic, season with salt and pepper, and cook for 1 minute. Pour in 1 cup (8 fl oz/250 ml) of the broth and stir to scrape up any browned bits on the pan bottom. Transfer the contents of the pan to a slow cooker and stir in the drained beans, remaining 3 cups (24 fl oz/750 ml) broth, the vinegar, pepper flakes to taste, bay leaves, and chorizo. Cover and cook on the low setting for 6–8 hours, stirring once or twice. The beans should be very tender.

Discard the bay leaves. Season with salt, pepper, and Tabasco. If desired, using the back of a spoon, mash some of the beans against the inside of the cooker to thicken the stew.

Spoon rice into shallow bowls, top with the stew, and serve.

CHILE VERDE

serves 8–10

4 lb (2 kg) boneless pork shoulder, cut into 1-inch (2.5-cm) chunks

Salt and freshly ground pepper

4 cans (7 oz/220 g each) diced fire-roasted green chiles

2 cans (12 oz/375 g each) whole tomatillos, drained and broken up by hand

1 large yellow onion, finely chopped

4 cloves garlic, minced

1 large jalapeño chile, seeded and minced

2 cups (16 fl oz/500 ml) chicken broth

¾ lb (375 g) ripe tomatoes, seeded and finely chopped

1 Tbsp dried oregano

2 tsp ground cumin

Warmed corn tortillas for serving

Sour cream for garnish

Chopped fresh cilantro for garnish

Put the pork in a large, heavy pot and season with 2 tsp salt and 1 tsp pepper. Add the green chiles, tomatillos, onion, garlic, jalapeño, broth, tomatoes, oregano, and cumin and stir briefly to combine. Bring to a boil over high heat, reduce the heat to very low, partially cover, and cook until the pork is very tender and a thick sauce has formed, 2–3 hours.

Ladle the chile verde into a large shallow serving bowl. Pass the tortillas, sour cream, and cilantro at the table.

BAKED GNOCCHI WITH TALEGGIO, PANCETTA & SAGE

serves 4

Pick up packs of fresh gnocchi, the little potato dumplings, to create easy—but filling—dinners in a pinch. They are lovely boiled until tender and simply sauced, but easily dressed up in a gratin, featuring decadent Italian bacon and cheeses. You can also make this recipe using 1 lb (500 g) penne or rigatoni instead of gnocchi.

Butter for dish

2 packages (13 oz/410 g each) prepared gnocchi

¼ lb (125 g) pancetta, cut into ½-inch (12-mm) pieces

2 Tbsp chopped fresh sage

1½ cups (12 fl oz/375 ml) half-and-half

½ lb (250 g) Taleggio cheese, rind removed, cut into ¼-inch (6-mm) cubes

¼ cup (1 oz/30 g) bread crumbs, toasted

Freshly ground pepper

Preheat the oven to 375°F (190°C). Butter four 7-inch (18-cm) shallow oval baking dishes.

Cook the gnocchi according to the package directions. Drain and set aside.

In a large frying pan, sauté the pancetta over medium heat until it starts to brown, about 4 minutes. Remove from the heat and stir in the sage, half-and-half, Taleggio, and gnocchi.

Divide the gnocchi mixture among the prepared dishes. Sprinkle with the bread crumbs and season with pepper.

Bake the gnocchi until golden brown, about 15 minutes. Remove from the oven and serve.

Golden brown
and bubbling,
this perennial
dish is welcome
at the table any
time of year.
Sweet Italian
sausage, colorful
peppers, and
fragrant fennel
add heft to this
one-pan baked
pasta. A touch of
cream finishes the
dish and rounds
out the tangy
tomato sauce.

BAKED RIGATONI WITH FENNEL, SAUSAGE & PEPERONATA

serves 6

2 Tbsp olive oil, plus more for greasing

Salt and freshly ground pepper

1 lb (500 g) rigatoni

1 fennel bulb

¾ lb (350 g) sweet Italian sausage, casings removed, crumbled

1 *each* red, yellow, and orange bell pepper, seeded and cut into matchsticks

1 tsp sugar

1 Tbsp red wine vinegar

1 cup (8 fl oz/250 ml) prepared tomato sauce

1½ cups (12 fl oz/375 ml) heavy cream

2 cups (8 oz/250 g) shredded fontina cheese

¼ cup (1 oz/30 g) grated Parmesan

Preheat the oven to 425°F (220°C). Lightly oil a 9-by-13-inch (24-by-33-cm) baking dish.

Bring a pot of salted water to a boil. Add the pasta and cook until al dente, 7–8 minutes, or according to the package directions. Drain and place in a large bowl.

Remove and discard the stalks and core from the fennel bulb and dice the bulb. In a frying pan, heat 1 Tbsp of the oil over medium heat. Add the crumbled sausage and cook, stirring occasionally, until lightly browned, 3–4 minutes. Add the fennel and cook, stirring, until tender, 4–5 minutes. Add to the bowl with the pasta.

Add the remaining 1 Tbsp oil to the pan, along with the bell peppers and a pinch each of salt and pepper. Cook, stirring occasionally, until the bell peppers are tender with a bit of a bite, 3–4 minutes. Add the sugar and vinegar and continue cooking until the vinegar has reduced to a syrup, 1–2 minutes. Add the tomato sauce and heavy cream and cook, stirring, until lightly thickened, 4–5 minutes. Transfer to the bowl with the pasta, add the fontina, and stir well.

Pour the pasta mixture into the prepared dish and top with the Parmesan. Bake until the top is golden brown and the sauce is bubbling around the sides, 10–15 minutes. Serve directly from the dish.

LAMB

CITRUS-BRAISED LAMB SHANKS

Lamb shanks meet a bright trio of citrus—lemon, lime, and orange—in this dish. The rich braising liquid that results from the slow cooking almost surpasses the lamb shanks themselves. If you want to stretch the recipe to serve six, shred the meat from the bones, divide among shallow bowls, and serve over rice, orzo, or polenta, with the reduced juices drizzled over each serving.

serves 4

2 Tbsp olive oil

4 lamb shanks, about 1 lb (500 g) each

Salt and freshly ground pepper

1 carrot, finely chopped

1 yellow onion, finely chopped

2 celery ribs, finely chopped

3 small sprigs fresh thyme

1 bay leaf

3 cloves garlic, minced

1½ Tbsp tomato paste

2 cups (16 fl oz/500 ml) dry white wine

1 cup (8 fl oz/250 ml) chicken broth

Grated zest and juice of 1 lemon

Grated zest and juice of 1 lime

Grated zest and juice of 1 orange

In a large, heavy pot, heat 1 Tbsp of the oil over medium-high heat. Season the shanks with salt and pepper. Working in batches, sear the shanks, turning as needed, until browned on all sides, 6–8 minutes. Transfer to a platter and pour off the fat from the pot.

Preheat the oven to 250°F (120°C). Add the remaining 1 Tbsp oil to the pot and place over medium-low heat. Add the carrot, onion, and celery and sauté until softened, about 5 minutes. Add the thyme, bay leaf, garlic, and tomato paste. Stir in ½ tsp salt, season with pepper, and stir for 1 minute. Add the wine, broth, and lemon and lime zests and juices.

Return the shanks to the pot and bring the liquid to a gentle simmer. Cover and cook in the oven, turning the shanks every hour, until the meat is completely tender, about 2½ hours. Transfer the shanks to a platter and keep warm in the oven.

Pour the juices from the pot into a large, heatproof measuring pitcher and let stand for 1 minute. The fat will rise to the top. Use a bulb baster to transfer the juices underneath the fat to a small saucepan. Simmer to reduce slightly. Stir in the orange zest and juice.

Drizzle the reduced juices over the lamb shanks and serve.

BRAISED MOROCCAN LAMB CHOPS

serves 6–8

¼ cup (1½ oz/45 g) **all-purpose flour**

Salt and freshly ground pepper

4 lb (2 kg) lamb shoulder chops, each about 1 inch (2.5 cm) thick

3 Tbsp olive oil

1 yellow onion, finely chopped

1 tsp ground cumin

1 tsp paprika

2 cups (16 fl oz/500 ml) beef broth

Juice of 1 lemon

1½ cups (7½ oz/235 g) green olives, pitted if desired

½ cup (¾ oz/20 g) minced fresh mint

On a large plate, stir together the flour and 1 tsp salt. Coat the lamb chops evenly with the flour mixture, shaking off the excess; reserve the remaining flour mixture. In a large frying pan, heat the oil over medium-high heat. Working in batches, sear the lamb chops, turning once, until browned, about 3 minutes. Transfer to a slow cooker.

Pour off all but about 1 Tbsp fat from the frying pan and return the pan to medium-high heat. Add the onion and sauté until translucent, 2–3 minutes. Sprinkle with the cumin, paprika, and reserved flour mixture and sauté briefly, just until fragrant. Pour in the broth and lemon juice. Raise the heat to high, bring to a boil, and stir to scrape up any browned bits on the pan bottom. Pour the contents of the pan over the lamb.

Cover and cook on the high setting for 3–4 hours or the low setting for 6–8 hours. The lamb should be very tender. About 1 hour before the lamb is done, add the olives. When the lamb is ready, transfer it to a platter and cover with foil to keep warm. Skim any fat from the surface of the braising liquid. Season with salt and pepper and stir in the mint. Spoon the sauce over the lamb and serve.

The best shepherd's pie starts with a languorously simmered lamb stew, fragrant with rosemary and a hint of garlic. Capped with creamy mashed potatoes, the topping becomes golden brown in the oven. Ask for boneless lamb shoulder at the meat counter, or if you like, substitute beef stew meat for a "cottage" pie.

SHEPHERD'S PIE

serves 6

2 lb (1 kg) boneless lamb shoulder, cut into 1-inch (2.5-cm) chunks

Salt and freshly ground pepper

2 Tbsp olive oil, plus more for greasing

8 Tbsp (4 oz/125 g) unsalted butter

1 large yellow onion, chopped

3 carrots, chopped

3 celery ribs, chopped

2 small cloves garlic, minced

⅓ cup (2 oz/60 g) all-purpose flour

3⅓ cups (27 fl oz/840 ml) beef broth

⅔ cup (5 fl oz/160 ml) dry white wine

2 tsp minced fresh rosemary

3 lb (1.5 kg) russet potatoes, peeled and cut into chunks

About ⅓ cup (3 fl oz/80 ml) heavy cream, warmed

1 cup (5 oz/155 g) fresh or thawed frozen peas

Preheat the oven to 325°F (165°C). Season the lamb with salt and pepper. In a large ovenproof pot, heat the oil over medium-high heat. Working in batches, sear the lamb, turning, until browned on all sides, about 5 minutes. Transfer to a plate.

In the same pot, melt 4 Tbsp of the butter over medium heat. Add the onion, carrots, celery, and garlic, cover, and cook, stirring, until the carrots are tender-crisp, about 5 minutes. Uncover, sprinkle with the flour, and stir well. Gradually stir in the broth and wine. Add the rosemary. Bring to a boil over medium heat, stirring to scrape up any browned bits from the pot bottom. Return the lamb to the pot, cover, place in the oven, and cook until the lamb is tender, 1½ hours.

About 30 minutes before the lamb is ready, oil a 3-qt (3-l) baking dish. In a saucepan, combine the potatoes with salted water to cover and bring to a boil. Reduce the heat to medium, and simmer until the potatoes are tender, 20–25 minutes. Drain well. Return the potatoes to the pan and stir over medium-low heat for 2 minutes to evaporate the excess moisture. Cut 3 Tbsp of the butter into pieces and add to the potatoes. Using a potato masher, mash the potatoes while adding enough cream to create a smooth mixture. Season with salt and pepper.

Season the lamb mixture with salt and pepper, stir in the peas, and pour into the prepared dish. Spread the mashed potatoes evenly on top. Cut the remaining 1 Tbsp butter into bits and use to dot the top. With the oven still at 325°F (165°C), bake until the top is lightly tinged with brown, about 20 minutes. Remove from the oven and let stand for about 5 minutes before serving.

POULTRY

SUMMER COQ AU VIN

Using white wine instead of the usual red transforms this slowly simmered stew into a lighter, fresher-tasting dish. If you like, garnish each serving with croutons made by sautéing cubes of crustless, good-quality white bread in a little olive oil until golden. Serve the dish with the same white wine you used to cook it.

serves 6–8

3 Tbsp all-purpose flour

Salt and ground pepper

4 lb (2 kg) assorted chicken pieces, skin on and bone in

3 Tbsp olive oil

4 shallots, minced

2 cups (16 fl oz/500 ml) dry white wine

1 cup (8 fl oz/250 ml) chicken broth

3 sprigs fresh flat-leaf parsley

2 sprigs fresh thyme

½ lb (250 g) summer squash, such as yellow crookneck or zucchini, cut into bite-sized pieces

3 carrots, cut into bite-sized pieces

¼ lb (125 g) frozen pearl onions, or 1 yellow onion, chopped

¼ lb (125 g) sugar snap peas, trimmed (optional)

On a plate, stir together the flour, 1 tsp salt, and ½ tsp pepper. Turn the chicken pieces in the seasoned flour, shaking off any excess. In a large, heavy pot, warm the oil over medium-high heat. Working in batches, sear the chicken, turning once, until browned, about 10 minutes. Transfer to a plate.

Add the shallots to the pot and cook over medium-high heat for about 30 seconds. Add the wine and stir to scrape up any browned bits on the pot bottom. Pour in the broth and bring to a boil.

Add the chicken to the pot, arranging the dark meat on the bottom and the breasts on top. Tuck the parsley and thyme sprigs among the chicken pieces. Reduce the heat to low, cover, and cook until the chicken is tender and opaque throughout, about 40 minutes. Uncover and add the squash, carrots, onions, and sugar snap peas (if using), pushing them into the cooking liquid around the chicken. Cover and cook until the vegetables are cooked through, about 20 minutes. Serve directly from the pot.

CHICKEN WITH BEANS, BACON & CHEDDAR

serves 4

1 Tbsp olive oil

4 skin-on whole chicken legs

Salt and freshly ground pepper

4 slices thick-cut bacon

1 small yellow onion, chopped

3 cloves garlic, minced

2 cans (15 oz/470 g each) pinto beans, rinsed and drained

2 plum tomatoes, chopped

2 Tbsp chopped fresh flat-leaf parsley

½ cup (2 oz/60 g) grated white Cheddar cheese

Preheat the oven to 400°F (200°C).

In a large, ovenproof frying pan, heat the oil over medium-high heat. Season the chicken legs with salt and pepper. Add to the pan, skin side down, and cook until browned, about 5 minutes. Turn and cook until almost cooked through, about 5 minutes more. Transfer to a plate.

Return the pan to medium-high heat, arrange the bacon slices in a single layer, and fry until crispy, about 7 minutes, turning once. Drain on paper towels, then break into big pieces.

Add the onion and garlic to the pan and sauté over medium-high heat until soft, 5 minutes. Add the beans and tomatoes and cook until the tomatoes begin to release their juices, about 3 minutes. Stir in the parsley and bacon and season with salt and pepper.

Return the chicken to the pan, nestling the pieces in the bean mixture. Sprinkle with the Cheddar. Cook in the oven until the cheese browns and the chicken is opaque throughout, about 10 minutes. Spoon onto plates or serve directly from the pan.

SUMMER CHICKEN BRAISE WITH WAX BEANS & TOMATOES

The colors of burnished chicken, yellow beans, red tomatoes, and green arugula make for a show-stopping presentation. Use a skillet or Dutch oven that you can bring straight to the table, and serve the chicken in shallow bowls to include the mustardy pan sauce. Offer plenty of warm crusty bread, and encourage guests to soak up every last drop.

serves 4

2 Tbsp olive oil

2 lb (1 kg) skin-on, bone-in chicken thighs and drumsticks

Salt and freshly ground pepper

1 yellow onion, chopped

1 carrot, chopped

6 cloves garlic, minced

1¼ cups (10 fl oz/310 ml) dry white wine

3 cups (24 fl oz/750 ml) chicken broth

3 sprigs fresh thyme

¼ cup (2 fl oz/60 ml) heavy cream

3 Tbsp Dijon mustard

1 cup (6 oz/185 g) cherry tomatoes

4 oz (125 g) small yellow wax beans

2 cups (3 oz/90 g) arugula leaves

Preheat the oven to 350°F (180°C).

In a large, heavy pot or a deep skillet, warm the oil over medium-high heat. Season the chicken with salt and pepper. Working in batches, sear the chicken, turning as needed, until browned, about 8 minutes. Transfer to a plate.

Add the onion, carrot, and garlic to the pot and season with salt and pepper. Sauté over medium-high heat until the vegetables soften, about 5 minutes. Add the wine, bring to a simmer, and cook until reduced by half, about 5 minutes. Add the broth and bring to a boil. Return the chicken to the pot, add the thyme, cover, and cook in the oven until the chicken is opaque throughout, about 55 minutes.

Transfer the chicken to a plate. Strain the braising liquid and return to the pot. Bring the liquid to a boil over high heat and cook until reduced by half, about 8 minutes. Reduce the heat to medium-high, stir in the cream and mustard, and cook until the sauce thickens, about 5 minutes. Season with salt and pepper. Arrange the chicken pieces in the pot, cover, and cook over low heat for 15 minutes to develop the flavors. Add the tomatoes and wax beans and cook, covered, until softened, about 5 minutes. Uncover, add the arugula, stir into the sauce, and cook just until wilted, about 1 minute. Serve directly from the pan.

Baby artichokes require some trimming, but you won't need to wrestle with removing the choke, which is negligible in the small vegetables. The rewards will be well worth your efforts. Out of season, you can use 1½ cups (12 oz/375 g) thawed, frozen hearts or drained marinated hearts, and add them with the tomatoes.

BRAISED CHICKEN & ARTICHOKES

serves 4–6

1 lemon, halved

1 lb (500 g) baby artichokes

3 Tbsp all-purpose flour

Salt and freshly ground pepper

2 *each* skinless, bone-in chicken breast halves, thighs, and drumsticks

2 Tbsp olive oil

4 cloves garlic, slivered

1 shallot, slivered

1 Tbsp *each* minced fresh basil, tarragon, and flat-leaf parsley

1 Tbsp Dijon mustard

1 cup (8 fl oz/250 ml) dry white wine

½ cup (4 fl oz/125 ml) chicken broth

3 plum tomatoes, seeded and chopped

Fill a large bowl with water and add the juice of ½ lemon. Trim the stem of each artichoke. Snap off the outer leaves until you reach the tender inner leaves. Cut off the top one-third of the artichoke. Halve each artichoke lengthwise, and if they seem large, cut each half in half. Add the artichokes to the lemon water.

Spread the flour on a plate, season well with salt and pepper, then lightly toss the chicken in the seasoned flour, shaking off the excess. In a large frying pan, heat the oil over medium-high heat. Add the chicken and cook, turning once, until lightly browned, 4–6 minutes. Transfer to a platter, and season with salt and pepper.

Pour off all but 2 Tbsp fat from the pan. Add the garlic and shallot and sauté until softened, 1–2 minutes. Stir in the herbs and mustard. Add the wine and broth, bring to a boil, and stir to scrape up any browned bits on the pan bottom. Add the tomatoes.

Return the thighs and drumsticks to the pan, reduce the heat to medium, and simmer for 10 minutes. Add the breasts and cook for another 10 minutes. Drain the artichokes, add to the pan, and cook until the chicken is opaque throughout and the artichokes are tender, about 10 minutes. Transfer to a deep platter and serve.

BRAISED CHICKEN WITH SHALLOTS & MUSHROOMS

Shallots break ground in spring. The purple-hued bulbs have a flavor somewhere between onion and garlic, and they braise to a delectable sweetness. White wine and tarragon enliven the pot, and dried mushrooms provide an earthy undertone.

serves 4–6

4½ lb (2.25 kg) assorted chicken pieces, preferably drumsticks and thighs

Salt and freshly ground pepper

3 Tbsp olive oil

6–8 shallots, chopped

3 cloves garlic, chopped

1 bottle (750 ml) full-bodied white wine

3 Tbsp small pieces dried mushrooms, such as chanterelle or porcini

2 cups (16 fl oz/500 ml) chicken broth

2 Tbsp coarsely chopped fresh tarragon

¾ cup (6 fl oz/180 ml) heavy cream

A few drops fresh lemon juice (optional)

2 Tbsp chopped fresh chives

1–2 Tbsp chopped fresh chervil or flat-leaf parsley

Preheat the oven to 350°F (180°C). Season the chicken pieces with salt and pepper, then rub with the oil. Heat a large, heavy frying pan over medium-high heat. Working in batches, sear the chicken, turning occasionally, until brown, 10–15 minutes. Transfer to a platter.

Pour off all but 1 Tbsp fat from the pan and place over medium heat. Add the shallots and garlic and sauté until softened, about 5 minutes. Add the wine, raise the heat to high, bring to a boil, and cook until reduced by half, 10–15 minutes. Stir in the mushrooms, broth, and half of the tarragon. Pour the sauce into a deep roasting pan large enough to hold the chicken in a single layer. Arrange the chicken in the sauce. Cook in the oven until the chicken is opaque throughout, 35–40 minutes.

Raise the heat to 400°F (200°C) and cook until the edges of the skin are crisp, about 5 minutes. Transfer to a deep platter and tent with foil.

Skim the fat from the surface of the sauce. Place the pan over high heat, bring the sauce to a boil, and cook, stirring, until reduced by about half, 7–8 minutes. Stir in the cream. Adjust the seasoning with salt and pepper and with lemon juice, if using. Pour the sauce over the chicken. Sprinkle with the chives, chervil, and remaining tarragon, and serve.

BRAISED CHICKEN WITH TANGERINE & STAR ANISE

serves 4

2 tangerines

8 skin-on, bone-in chicken thighs, about 3¼ lb (1.6 kg) total

Salt and freshly ground pepper

2 Tbsp peanut oil

1 small yellow onion, finely chopped

2 cloves garlic, minced

1 tsp peeled and grated fresh ginger

1 cup (8 fl oz/250 ml) chicken broth

2 Tbsp soy sauce

1 tsp chile-garlic sauce, such as Sriracha

2–3 star anise

2 tsp cornstarch dissolved in 1 Tbsp water

Finely grate the zest from the tangerines, then squeeze ½ cup (4 fl oz/125 ml) juice. Season the chicken with 1 tsp salt and ½ tsp pepper.

In a large, heavy pot, heat the oil over medium-high heat. Working in batches, sear the chicken, turning once or twice, until browned on both sides, about 9 minutes. Transfer to a plate.

Pour off all but 1 Tbsp fat in the pot and return the pot to medium heat. Add the onion and cook, stirring occasionally, until softened, 3–4 minutes. Add the garlic, the ginger, and half of the tangerine zest and stir until fragrant, about 1 minute. Add the broth, tangerine juice, soy sauce, chile-garlic sauce, and star anise and bring to a boil, stirring to scrape up any browned bits from the bottom of the pot. Return the chicken to the pot, reduce the heat to low, cover, and simmer until the chicken is opaque throughout, about 25 minutes.

Transfer the chicken to a platter. Bring the liquid in the pot to a boil over medium-high heat. Stir in the cornstarch mixture and cook just until the sauce thickens slightly, about 30 seconds.

Pour the sauce over the chicken. Sprinkle with the remaining tangerine zest and serve.

PORTER-BRAISED CHICKEN WITH ROOT VEGETABLES

Slightly bitter and with a deep coffee-like flavor, porter, a very dark ale, makes this braise rustic and hearty. Porter's toastiness plus the sweetness of root vegetables and the spiciness of Dijon mustard creates a stew full of contrasting, but harmonious, flavors. Top with fresh chopped parsley for a colorful garnish.

serves 4

8 skin-on, bone-in chicken thighs, about 3½ lb (1.75 kg) total

Salt and freshly ground pepper

2 Tbsp canola oil

2 Tbsp unsalted butter, plus 5 Tbsp (2½ oz/75 g) at room temperature

1 large yellow onion, chopped

2 carrots, cut into 1-inch (2.5-cm) chunks

2 red potatoes, cut into 1-inch (2.5-cm) chunks

1 celery root, about 14 oz (440 g), peeled, trimmed, halved, and cut into 1-inch (2.5-cm) chunks

2 bottles (12 fl oz/375 ml each) porter

2 cups (16 fl oz/500 ml) chicken broth

2 Tbsp packed light brown sugar

2 Tbsp Dijon mustard

2 tsp tomato paste

1 tsp dried thyme

⅓ cup (2 oz/60 g) all-purpose flour

Season the chicken thighs with salt and pepper. In a large, heavy pot, heat the oil over medium-high heat. Working in batches, sear the chicken thighs, turning once or twice, until lightly browned on both sides, about 5 minutes. Transfer to a plate. Pour off the fat in the pot.

Reduce the heat to medium and melt the 2 Tbsp butter. Add the onion and sauté until golden, about 6 minutes. Add the carrots, potatoes, and celery root, and stir in the porter, broth, sugar, mustard, tomato paste, and thyme. Return the chicken thighs to the pot, submerging them in the liquid, and bring to a simmer. Cover, reduce the heat to medium-low, and simmer, stirring occasionally, for 30 minutes.

In a heatproof bowl, mash together the 5 Tbsp butter and the flour to form a thick paste. Gradually whisk about 2 cups (16 fl oz/500 ml) of the hot cooking liquid into the flour-butter mixture, and then stir this mixture into the pot. Cover and simmer, stirring occasionally, until the chicken is opaque throughout, about 10 minutes. Adjust the seasoning and serve.

BRAISED CHICKEN WITH TOMATILLOS & CILANTRO

serves 6

3 Anaheim or poblano chiles

2 Tbsp canola oil

3½ lb (1.75 kg) assorted chicken pieces, skin on and bone in

1 large yellow onion, finely chopped

2 cups (16 fl oz/500 ml) chicken broth

6 cloves garlic, minced

1½ lb (750 g) tomatillos, husked and cut into quarters *(left)*

3 Tbsp finely chopped fresh cilantro, plus whole leaves for garnish

½ tsp ground cumin

1 Tbsp fresh lime juice

Salt and freshly ground pepper

Warm tortillas for serving

Preheat the broiler. Place the chiles on a baking sheet and broil, turning them with tongs, until blackened on all sides. Transfer to a paper bag, close tightly, and let stand for 10 minutes. Peel the chiles, remove the stems, seeds, and ribs, and finely chop the chiles. Set aside.

In a large sauté pan with a lid, heat the oil over medium-high heat. Working in batches, sear the chicken, turning once, until browned, 7–8 minutes. Transfer to a plate.

Reduce the heat to medium and add the onion and sauté until softened, 3–5 minutes. Add the broth, stirring to scrape up any browned bits on the pan bottom. Add the roasted chiles, garlic, tomatillos, chopped cilantro, and cumin. Bring to a boil, then reduce the heat to low. Return the chicken and any juices to the pan, cover, and simmer, turning once, until the chicken is opaque throughout, about 20 minutes. The white meat and smaller pieces will be done first. Transfer the chicken to a platter and tent with foil to keep warm.

Add the lime juice to the pan and cook the sauce over high heat until slightly reduced and thickened. Season with salt and pepper. Pour the sauce over the chicken and garnish with the cilantro leaves. Serve with the tortillas alongside.

CHICKEN STUFFED WITH SPINACH & CHEESE

Butterflied chicken breasts turn into a simple yet elegant meal when stuffed with a filling of tangy goat cheese and earthy spinach. Paper-thin strips of prosciutto help to package it all together and crisp up into a deliciously salty exterior. These bundles are delicious on their own or alongside a simple orzo and cherry tomato salad.

serves 4

Oil for dish

2 cups (2 oz/60 g) baby spinach, chopped

¼ lb (125 g) fresh goat cheese, crumbled

½ cup (2 oz/60 g) grated Parmesan cheese

Salt and freshly ground pepper

4 skinless, boneless chicken breast halves, about 1½ lb (750 g) total

4 large, thin slices prosciutto or cooked ham

Preheat the oven to 400°F (200°C). Oil a shallow baking dish just large enough to hold the chicken breasts in a single layer. In a bowl, mix together the spinach, goat cheese, and Parmesan. Season with salt and pepper.

Place each chicken breast on a work surface. Holding a sharp knife parallel to the work surface, cut each breast in half lengthwise almost all the way through. Spread one-fourth of the spinach-cheese mixture in the center of each breast. Fold the chicken breast closed and season with salt and pepper. Wrap 1 prosciutto slice tightly around each chicken breast and place in the prepared dish.

Bake until the prosciutto is crisp and the chicken is opaque throughout, about 20 minutes. Serve directly from the dish.

STIR-FRIED CHICKEN WITH SUGAR SNAP PEAS & LEMON

serves 4–6

2 skinless, boneless chicken breast halves, about 6 oz (185 g) each

Salt and freshly ground pepper

1 lemon

1 cup (8 fl oz/250 ml) chicken broth

2 Tbsp Asian fish sauce

1 tsp sugar

1 tsp cornstarch

4 Tbsp (2 fl oz/60 ml) peanut or grapeseed oil

2 green onions, white and tender green parts chopped, green tops thinly sliced

½-inch (12-mm) piece peeled fresh ginger, grated

2 cloves garlic, minced

½ lb (250 g) sugar snap peas, trimmed

3 Tbsp coarsely chopped fresh mint

Cut the chicken across the grain on a slight diagonal into slices about ½ inch (12 mm) thick. Season with 1 tsp salt and ¼ tsp pepper.

Grate the zest from the lemon, and then squeeze 2 Tbsp juice. In a small nonreactive bowl, stir together the broth, fish sauce, sugar, and lemon zest and juice. In another small bowl, mix the cornstarch with 1 Tbsp cold water.

In a wok or very large frying pan, heat 2 Tbsp of the oil over medium-high heat until hot. Add the chicken and stir-fry until opaque throughout, about 3 minutes. Transfer to a plate. Return the pan to medium-high heat, add the remaining 2 Tbsp oil, and heat until very hot but not smoking. Add the chopped green onions, ginger, and garlic and stir-fry until fragrant, about 15 seconds. Add the sugar snap peas and ¼ cup (2 oz/60 ml) water, cover, and cook, stirring occasionally, until the peas turn bright green, about 1 minute.

Return the chicken to the pan and add the sliced green onions and the mint. Stir the broth mixture, add to the pan, and bring to a boil, stirring constantly. Stir the cornstarch mixture, stir into the pan, and cook until the sauce is slightly thickened, about 15 seconds. Adjust the seasoning and serve.

ARROZ CON POLLO

serves 6

4 large cloves garlic, minced

2 tsp red pepper flakes

1 Tbsp white vinegar

Salt and freshly ground pepper

3 lb (1.5 kg) chicken pieces, skin on and bone in

3 Tbsp olive oil

4 cups (32 fl oz/1 l) chicken broth

½ tsp saffron threads

1 red onion, chopped

2 bell peppers, seeded and chopped

1 large jalapeño chile, seeded and minced

4 plum tomatoes, chopped

1 tsp ground cumin

2 bay leaves

2 cups (14 oz/440 g) long-grain white rice

In a large bowl, stir together the garlic, red pepper flakes, vinegar, 1 tsp salt, and ½ tsp pepper. Add the chicken pieces, toss to coat, and refrigerate for at least 1 hour or up to overnight.

In a large frying pan with a lid, heat the oil over medium heat. Remove the chicken and brush off the marinade, reserving it in the bowl. Arrange the chicken in the pan, skin side down, and cook without turning, until golden brown, 10–15 minutes. Turn the chicken, cover the pan, and cook until golden on the second side, about 10 minutes. Meanwhile, in a saucepan, warm the broth over medium-high heat. Remove from the heat, crumble in the saffron, and let steep.

Transfer the chicken to a plate and pour off all but 2 Tbsp fat from the pan. Add the onion, bell peppers, and jalapeño and sauté until softened, about 3 minutes. Add the tomatoes and cook, stirring, for 1 minute. Add the cumin, bay leaves, and rice and cook, stirring constantly, until the rice has absorbed the pan juices, 3–5 minutes. Pour the reserved marinade and saffron broth into the pan and stir briefly. Place the chicken on top. Raise the heat to medium-high and bring to a boil. Reduce the heat to low, cover, and simmer until the chicken is opaque throughout, the rice is tender, and the liquid has been absorbed, about 25 minutes. Let stand for 5–10 minutes before serving.

TURKEY TETRAZZINI

serves 6–8

Olive oil for greasing

7 Tbsp (3½ oz/105 g) unsalted butter

2 shallots, minced

½ lb (250 g) button mushrooms, sliced

⅓ cup (2 oz/60 g) all-purpose flour

3 cups (24 fl oz/750 ml) chicken broth

Salt and ground white pepper

3 cups (18 oz/560 g) shredded cooked turkey

½ lb (250 g) egg noodles, cooked according to package directions

¾ cup (3 oz/90 g) grated Parmesan cheese

2 green onions, white and tender green parts, chopped

1 cup (2 oz/60 g) fresh bread crumbs

This retro casserole uses up leftover turkey in a tangle of egg noodles, button mushrooms, and cheesy sauce—with delicious results. Baked in one pan, or divided into individual ramekins, it is sure to become an annual post-holiday tradition. Use both white and dark turkey meat, as the dark meat will add moisture.

Preheat the oven to 450°F (230°C). Oil a 9-by-13-inch (23-by-33-cm) baking dish or 6 individual ramekins or baking dishes.

In a large frying pan, melt 2 Tbsp of the butter over medium-high heat. Add the shallots and mushrooms and sauté until the mushrooms begin to brown, about 5 minutes. Transfer to a large bowl.

Add 4 Tbsp of the butter to the pan and melt over medium-high heat. Add the flour and cook, stirring constantly, for 2 minutes. Add the broth and bring to a boil. Cook, stirring frequently, until the sauce thickens, about 4 minutes. Season with 1 tsp salt and ½ tsp pepper. Pour the sauce into the bowl with the mushrooms and add the turkey, the cooked noodles, ½ cup (2 oz/60g) of the Parmesan, and the green onions and stir to combine.

In a small bowl, mix the bread crumbs with the remaining ¼ cup (1 oz/30 g) Parmesan.

Transfer the turkey mixture to the prepared dish(es). Sprinkle evenly with the bread crumb mixture. Using your fingers, break the remaining 1 Tbsp butter into small pieces and sprinkle over the top.

Bake until the tetrazzini is bubbly around the edges and the bread crumbs are golden brown, about 15 minutes. Serve.

CHICKEN TAGINE WITH PRESERVED LEMONS & OLIVES

This colorful Moroccan stew offers deep spices, but stays light and bright with tart citrus, briny green olives, and fresh cilantro. For the most authentic presentation, serve it on a platter or individual plates atop a bed of couscous.

serves 4

¼ tsp saffron threads

2 large yellow onions, chopped

½ cup (¾ oz/20 g) coarsely chopped fresh cilantro, plus more for garnish

½ cup (¾ oz/20 g) coarsely chopped fresh flat-leaf parsley, plus more for garnish

4 Tbsp (2 fl oz/60 ml) fresh lemon juice

1 tsp ground cumin

½ tsp ground ginger

½ tsp ground turmeric

Salt

2 large cloves garlic, crushed

6 Tbsp olive oil

6 skin-on, bone-in chicken thighs

2 preserved lemons, thinly sliced

½ cup (4 fl oz/125 ml) chicken broth

1½ cups (8 oz/250 g) cracked green olives

In a small bowl, soak the saffron in 2 Tbsp warm water for 10 minutes.

In a food processor, combine the onions, the ½ cup cilantro, ½ cup parsley, and 2 Tbsp of the lemon juice. Add the cumin, ginger, turmeric, and the saffron and its soaking liquid. Season with 1 tsp salt and process to a pulpy purée. Transfer to a large resealable plastic bag. Add the garlic and 3 Tbsp of the oil. Add the chicken pieces, seal the bag, and massage to coat the chicken with the mixture. Refrigerate for at least 8 hours or up to 24 hours.

In a large, heavy pot, warm 1 Tbsp of the oil over medium-high heat. Add the lemon slices and sear until browned, 3–5 minutes. Transfer to a plate. Add the remaining 2 Tbsp oil to the pot. Remove the chicken pieces from the marinade, shaking off the excess and reserving the marinade. Working in batches, sear the chicken pieces, skin side down, until golden brown, 5–6 minutes. Transfer to another plate.

Pour the broth into the pot, stirring to scrape up any browned bits from the pot bottom. Stir in the reserved marinade and add the chicken and any juices. Bring to a boil, cover, reduce the heat to medium-low, and simmer until the chicken is opaque throughout, about 40 minutes.

Simmer the olives in a saucepan of boiling water for 5 minutes. Add the olives, the reserved lemon, and the remaining 2 Tbsp lemon juice to the pot. Cover and simmer until the chicken is falling-off-the-bone tender, 10–15 minutes.

Garnish the stew with chopped cilantro and parsley and serve.